Only One Life is an encouraging read that confirms our significant role as women in the present day, as well as in history. The message is a powerful reminder that each decision and aspect of our lives shapes the future. It is refreshing to read these vivid stories of female impact!

—Lauren Scruggs Kennedy, author; blogger; founder,
Lauren Scruggs Kennedy Foundation

Only One Life is a beautiful reminder of the strength and resilience of women and the eternal legacy each generation leaves to the next. What a gift to be reminded that the callings we fulfill are because we stand on the shoulders of those women before us who stood for justice, righteousness, and compassion.

—Christine Caine, founder, A21 and Propel
Women; author, *Unexpected*

My friends Lauren and Jackie give us the stories of significant and persuasive women who, by their winsome examples, have won the right to be heard *and* followed. Thank you, Lauren and Jackie, for introducing us to the *real* movers and shakers in our world!

—Joni Eareckson Tada, Joni and Friends
International Disability Center

Jackie and Lauren have done a fantastic job telling the stories of courageous women who've inspired us for generations. Don't miss the invitation to read this book and leave an inspiring legacy of your own. You are already more influential than you think!

—Esther Fleece, speaker; author, *No More Faking Fine*

Only One Life is a "Wow!" because in reading Jackie and Lauren's book, you keep company with women from times past and present who came to know, love, and serve God and, like the Greens, want to leave a legacy "worthy of him who called us." There is much to be learned.

—Kay Arthur, teacher; author; cofounder,
Precept Ministries International

This mom and daughter duo motivates all women to live out abundantly more than we could ever dream of when we invite Jesus to take over. I'm certain this book, through the many stories it tells, will challenge anyone to dream bigger!

—Chelsea Crockett, author, *Your Own Beautiful*

Amid daily news of injustice against women, minorities, and children, Jackie and Lauren introduce us to real-life answers and the women who represent these answers. I honestly could not put this book down and will be using it as a reference for years to come.

—Lynette Lewis, business consultant; author,
Climbing the Ladder in Stilettos

Only One Life posts a needed challenge to the next generation of women of faith: What will be our legacy? This book inspired me greatly and showed me some powerful female role models. Lauren and Jackie put great time, effort, and thought into this book, and it shows. It is a gift.

—Megan Alexander, correspondent, *Inside Edition*; author, *Faith in the Spotlight*

I'm so glad for this book because stories of Christian women need to be told! Out of their conviction and obedience to God, these women led, pioneered, championed, raised, and taught in ways that have left an indelible mark on our world.

—Mai Hariu-Powell, executive director, The New York Project at Redeemer City to City

One Life to Live is a poignant reminder of the power each of us has to establish a legacy that will shape families, influence cultures, and ultimately change the entire world. This book is a gift. Read it and then go and establish a legacy of your own.

—Dr. Lois Evans and Priscilla Shirer (mother and daughter)

only one life

HOW A WOMAN'S

only

EVERY DAY

SHAPES AN ETERNAL

one

LEGACY

life

JACKIE GREEN AND LAUREN GREEN MCAFEE

WITH BILL HIGH

ZONDERVAN

Only One Life
Copyright © 2018 by Jackie Green, Lauren Green McAfee, Bill High

Requests for information should be addressed to:
Zondervan, *3900 Sparks Dr. SE, Grand Rapids, Michigan 49546*

ISBN 978-0-310-35171-9 (softcover)

ISBN 978-0-310-35329-4 (audio)

ISBN 978-0-310-35270-9 (ebook)

Authors are represented by The Christopher Ferebee Agency, www.christopherferebee.com.

Cover design: Tim Green | Faceout Studio
Interior design: Denise Froehlich

First printing April 2018 / Printed in the United States of America

FROM LAUREN

*To all the amazing women hoping
to make an eternal difference
through their everyday offerings.*

*And to my husband, Michael: you
make me a better woman.*

FROM JACKIE

*To women everywhere:
You were created for a special
purpose, and you spread light in this
world in a multitude of ways.*

*To my daughters, granddaughter,
and those to come:
Lauren, Lindy, Danielle, Grace,
Gabriella, Erica and Mary-Kate.*

*I feel incredibly blessed to have
each one of you in my life.*

CONTENTS

ACKNOWLEDGMENTS

FROM JACKIE

As I considered writing this book, I kept thinking about how absolutely blessed I am to have so many wonderful women in my life who have impacted and influenced me in all kinds of ways. Some of them are big influences, and some are subtle but have changed the course of my life or influenced my decisions. I am grateful for each and every one of the women who have been a part—big or small—of my journey. I couldn't possibly list every single one, but I would like to mention a few. Those I don't list, you know who you are. You are the ones who send me a text message of encouragement or an email that you are praying for me. Maybe you showed compassion and brought a meal when I was recovering from illness, shared wisdom and your faith, or taught me or my children in a class. There are those who stood tenaciously, boldly, and loyally by my side through ups and downs. I have witnessed your often unrecognized acts of generosity, thoughtful and serving care of others, and diligence to always be learning more about the Bible and being faithful to God. You have been a part of my life in some way as an example and I thank you. I will try to exemplify the character you have shown me and extend it to others.

To my mother, Nita, and my grandmothers, Delia and Vera: You poured your wisdom into me during my formative years and didn't ever give up on me. Mom, your balance of faith, wisdom, and love was just what I needed and such a wonderful gift from God. And many thanks to my mother-in-law, Barbara, who has been a motherly influence of faith to me in my adult years. I'm so grateful for the godly matriarchs in my life. Telling your story and sharing of God's faithfulness set me in the right direction.

To my five daughters, daughter-in-law, and granddaughter (Lauren, Lindy, Danielle, Grace, Gabi, Erica, Mary-Kate): My eyes fill with tears of joy and love when I think of you all. You are such amazing women and girls! I feel God hand-selected each of you—with your individual personalities, gifts, and strengths—to enrich my life and our family. Thank you for sacrificially cheering me on, for regular hugs, for being the best kids a mom could have, and for desiring to love the Lord your God with all your hearts, souls, and minds (Matt. 22:37–39).

To my extended family: So many strong, committed, responsible, gracious, talented, beautiful, loving, and kind women and men of integrity.

To the Claxton Family Quilt Guild: With special thanks to Brenda, Ashley, and Kristi for opening your lake homes. We have made some great laughter-filled memories together, as well as our collaborative quilt projects that we can cherish and pass down to future generations. I think we made Grannie proud, and Grandma Claxton would have loved it!

To my "therapy" prayer group and some of the finest friends a girl could experience life with: Bea, Cheri, Cindi, Connie, Denise, Ginger, Jaime, Jetta, Julie, Kathy B., Kathy T., Melanie, Peggy, Sarah, Stephanie, Teri, Tina, Traci, and Vickey. You show the character of Christ to me and others in so many ways! Who would have guessed that we would all get to have so much fun together as our kids grow up and our families expand? Weddings and baby showers, birthday celebrations, the annual Christmas luncheon, coffee talks, movie dates, and group texts with heartfelt love, encouragement, support, and prayer needs fill my heart with gladness. Also to my helpers, Ha, Makenzie, Trish, Marsha, and Dru: You *all* are great examples of how different talents work together to make a whole, fully functioning body (1 Cor. 12:26–27).

Last but definitely not least, I want to acknowledge the awesome men in my life. My father and father-in-law, Jack and David: You are hardworking and faith-filled examples. My son, sons-in-law, and grandsons (Derek, Michael, Caleb, Fenix, Cruz, and Luca): I'm so proud that you guys are strong in your faith. You work hard, serve, love, and lead our family well.

To my husband, Steve: For the past thirty-three years you have been the most influential human being in my life. You are my "other half," you lead our home with your solid example of following the Lord with your whole heart, and you offer strength or tenderness depending on what I need. I love the times we get to just be the teenage girl and boy who fell head over heels in love with each other! I love you to the moon and back!

To my Lord, my Rock, my Redeemer: without you I am nothing. With you, I am all I need to be.

FROM LAUREN

To my Creator: I have to start by acknowledging my Savior, Jesus Christ. God's gospel changed my life. It is only with the help of God through his Holy Spirit that it's possible to walk this path toward an eternal legacy.

To my mother: We have had different experiences in life, and we have different personalities. But we have the same passion for pursuing a lasting legacy and encouraging others along the way. The process of writing together has led me to have an even greater admiration for you as I watched you lean in and work hard to share inspiration and truth with authenticity and vulnerability. You never cease to amaze me. Mom, I love you. Thank you for making this book possible, in every way.

To my husband: You are my other half, and you make me a better woman. You constantly live out the gospel in our marriage and sacrificially lead me. You know me better than I know myself. I praise God for the gift that you are to me. I pray that our legacy together will always point others to God's great glory.

To the women in my family: There are so many inspiring women I am privileged to call family—the women in my life who have daily shaped me, challenged me, loved on me, and inspired me. I love you deeply. Your impact is written throughout my story. I don't know what I would do without you. My sisters, Lindy Green, Danielle Green Smith, Grace Green, Gabi Green, Erica Green, and Clytee McAfee: You are one of the greatest blessings in my life. You are my people. My mother-in-law, Terri McAfee: Your tenacity, compassion, and faith have significantly left their mark on one of my favorite humans: my husband. You have created an incredible legacy that inspires me. My grandmothers, Barbara Green and Nita Chartier: You are spectacular examples of living life on purpose and raising godly generations. To all of the women in my extended family too: You are each special to me in your own way.

To the many women in my life who have provided such sweet community throughout the various seasons of my life: Casey Y., Whitney F., Elizabeth F., Megan M., Ashley O., Asha M., Diandra T., Angel T., Kirsten H., Ruth M., Esther F., Jess R., Cherrie M., and so many others who walk alongside me in life, giving me strength and pointing me to Christ. And to the women who have been mentors, Raylee Butler and Millicent Gillogly: Thank you for being wonderful examples to me.

FROM JACKIE AND LAUREN

We also want to thank those who contributed to the publishing of this book:

- Tom Dean, Robin Barnett, and the amazing Zondervan team: We have loved working with you!
- Stephanie Smith: You were extremely encouraging as our

editor. Thank you for believing in us and making our book the best it could be!

- Bill High: You persuaded us to find the time to share a relevant message for women today. Your contributions were appreciated, as well as your efforts to understand the female perspective. Many thanks!
- Annika Bergen: Your tireless efforts to help us wrap up edits and final content were just what we needed.
- Bev Mansfield: For hearing what our hearts were trying to put into words and gifting us with the words on paper. You and the team at Chartwell Literary Group did a fabulous job!
- The inspiring women mentioned in this book who are still on their faith journeys: Kay Arthur, Sarah Bowling, Christine Caine, Mary Beth Chapman, Queen Elizabeth II, Amy Orr-Ewing, Barbara Green, Marilyn Hickey, Lauren Scruggs Kennedy, and Joni Eareckson Tada.

ONLY ONE LIFE: THE WAY OF LEGACY

Only one life.

Chances are you've never heard of her, but her impact for the gospel and for good is beyond calculation. And it's still expanding, encircling the globe even as you read these words. She passed away more than forty years ago, yet she continues to "outlive her life." Her name was Marie, and we both stand on the shoulders of this extraordinary woman.

Marie was born in Kansas City in 1903. The daughter of a pastor, she grew up and married a pastor as well. Together she and Walter Green raised six children through the austere years of the Great Depression and World War II on a preacher's meager income. Her children later recalled their years in a tiny parsonage, where the girls slept in the lone bedroom, the parents slept in the living room, and the boys bedded down each night in the kitchen. They recalled going to school without shoes until a few generous teachers quietly stepped in to help meet that need.

They experienced real hunger at times. Yet largely because of the extraordinary faith and influence of mother Marie, they remembered above all a home filled with love for each other and for God. Marie also modeled a heart of compassion for people who had no knowledge of a loving God or of the Son He sent to seek and save the lost. So amid her manifold responsibilities as a pastor's wife and mother, she somehow found time to crochet doilies and sell them to raise money for missions.

Marie's love for God was as contagious as it was strong. Not only did every one of her children embrace the biblical faith that anchored her soul, but also five of them either answered a call to full-time ministry or married a minister. It would be impossible to calculate the impact those five children have had on the eternal destinies of others—both directly through their personal witness and by extension as those they touched then touched others, in an ever-expanding web of blessing.

But what of that sixth child? The one who did not sense a call to a life of full-time ministry?

David Green was the next to youngest of Marie's children. He grew up to become my (Jackie's) father-in-law and my (Lauren's) grandfather. He too loved God and dedicated his life to following Him at an early age. But despite the heavy weight of expectations that must have enveloped him, given the choices of his older siblings, David knew in the depths of his soul that he was not called to be a minister in the traditional sense.

His gifts and passion led him into retail business instead. Perhaps Marie's crafty ingenuity of crocheting doilies and selling them to raise money for missionaries made a deeper impression on the young man than anyone could have imagined.

In 1970, he took a leap of faith with his wife, Barbara, and their young children in Oklahoma City and launched a new business from their kitchen table—initially assembling picture frames and wholesaling them to local retail stores. My (Jackie's) husband, Steve, was seven years old, and his parents paid him seven cents for each frame he glued together. Not long after, they launched their shop for artists and home crafters in a small storefront. They called it Hobby Lobby.

A move to a bigger location soon followed, and in the ensuing decades many other locations sprang up across America. You'll find the details of the amazing Hobby Lobby growth story in David Green's 2005 book *More Than a Hobby: How a $600 Start-up Became America's Home and Craft Superstore.* Today Hobby Lobby is one of our nation's most successful and healthy privately held companies, with more than eight hundred stores coast to coast and employing more than thirty-five thousand full- and part-time workers.

However, Hobby Lobby's amazing business success is only a sliver of the story. The best part is the one David Green is least comfortable talking about—his and his company's commitment to evangelism and Christian philanthropy. Here's how *Forbes* magazine described Marie Green's second-to-youngest child in a 2012 profile titled "Meet David Green: Hobby Lobby's Biblical Billionaire": "David Green insists God is the true owner of his $3 billion arts and crafts chain. Acting as His disciple, Green has become the largest evangelical benefactor in the world—with plans for unprecedented gifts once he's in heaven."[1]

The fact is that for years Hobby Lobby has taken half of all pretax earnings and poured the money into evangelistic outreaches, ministries, and humanitarian projects. Donations have flowed to an astonishing array of churches, Christian nonprofits, Christian colleges, and other gospel-advancing projects, as well as to organizations that dig water wells and provide medical care for third-world countries, to community events, adoption services—even to fund part of the Oklahoma City capitol dome! It's no accident that our father's/grandfather's latest book, released in 2017, is titled *Giving It All Away . . . and Getting It All Back Again: The Way of Living Generously.*

Please understand, we're not highlighting all this generosity and impact for the kingdom of God to glorify a person or a company. Rather let's trace the impact backward and turn the spotlight once again to Marie Green, the mother who taught and modeled those values and inspired her children to embrace them. When we take in the full picture, we see the lasting generational impact one godly woman can have, even an unassuming pastor's wife living in a small town.

Did Marie think about being a woman of legacy, a woman

who would pass down a spiritual heritage to her family? She may not have used those words, but there is no question she understood this vital concept. All of her children recall her citing a refrain from a poem by British missionary C. T. Studd titled "Only One Life." Each stanza ends with the line

> Only one life, 'twill soon be past,
> Only what's done for Christ will last.

She recited those lines to her children countless times, often in the context of engaging in a sacrificial act of love or service. Marie Green became a woman of legacy because she knew in the deepest depths of her heart what many believers in our time have forgotten, a truth enshrined in this quote from C. S. Lewis: "If you read history you will find that the Christians who did most for the present world were precisely those who thought most of the next."[2]

Marie Green moved to that glorious next world in 1975 and therefore didn't get to see the amazing Hobby Lobby story unfold. At that time, it was still just a fledgling company. Nevertheless, all of this and more is very much a part of our grandmother's/ great-grandmother's legacy.

A Woman's Legacy?

As we said, we are living, breathing evidence of the kind of impact a woman of faith can have on the world. Marie Green was a leader in a very real and important sense. Of course, our fractured nation and our hurting world need godly women leaders now more than ever. We can lead. We must lead. Future generations will bless us if we press through our obstacles, fears, and insecurities to meet the sobering challenges our families and communities now face.

What about you? Are you a woman of legacy?

The fact that you're holding this book right now strongly suggests that the answer to this question matters to you. The idea of leaving a legacy may sound intimidating. But legacy is not meant only for the elite few who have great power or influence. Legacy is crafted by our faithful everyday choices, and we hope to explore stories of women who prove that anyone can truly leave a lasting legacy—even you.

But what does *legacy* really mean? How does it impact our day-to-day lives? And perhaps the biggest question of all, Why does it really matter?

Before we dive into these questions, perhaps we should introduce ourselves!

The "we" asking these questions are a mother (Jackie) and a daughter (Lauren). We've traveled the road of so many women who assume roles of daughters, wives, and mothers, all the while wondering whether there might be something more. As a result of that journey, we've learned some hard and wonderful lessons that we can share with our fellow travelers.

No matter where you are in life, legacy is for every age and every season. Jackie is part of generation X, while Lauren is a millennial. Though we are from different generations, we both carry the same God-given burden for seeing Christian women recognize their capacity to leave positive, world-changing legacies that will continue to make the world a better place long after their time on earth is done.

We must admit we approach this topic with humility and trepidation because we are still on this journey of figuring out how to consistently invest in our legacies every day.

I (Jackie) grew up in a small town in Oklahoma and moved to the big capital city of our state when I married at eighteen years old. My husband, Steve, and I met at church camp when we were young teens, started dating my senior year of high school, married in August after I graduated in May, and never looked back. I never dreamed that my path would look like the one I have walked and still walk every day. As a teen, I had plans to climb the corporate ladder, but I married at eighteen and worked in the family business until I became a mother at twenty. I thought I would have three amazing kids, and I have six. I thought by the time I was in my forties, I would have all of my children raised and my husband and I would be taking leisurely vacations at least twice a year (I also had visions of being able to go to the gym or salon whenever I wanted, having every room in my home organized, and staying on top of the mail and paperwork that comes in by the loads when you have a large family).

My first child was born when I was twenty years old, and my youngest child was born when I was forty. My point is that we all have plans for our lives, and sometimes I wonder if God looks down on us, chuckles, and says, "Let's see if you want to know *My* plans for your life," as He guides us lovingly along a much different path.

I remember that when my youngest child started kindergarten, I prayed and pondered what path I wanted to take, now that I had a little more freedom with my time. What would I do with those extra hours? I thought about taking a photography class, hiring a physical trainer, and attending as many of the ladies' Bible studies as I wanted, but my life took another turn. That was the year the Museum of the Bible was established, and I found myself by my husband's side, called to launch a world-class museum inviting all people to engage with the Bible.

As we traveled together to around three hundred events over the last three years, I met so many marvelous women. Much of the time our stories had similarities. We wanted to live a life of integrity, serve our families and friends well, and utilize our time, talents, and treasures for God's kingdom purposes. Often busyness was our common enemy. I found myself wanting to encourage these women to be intentional with their busyness and use their gifts for things that really matter, realizing that as women, we have unique opportunities to impact the lives of those around us every single day. After all, as I've heard said before, our faith isn't handed down genetically; it's handed down personally.

I am at least halfway through my life's journey, and I want to be busy doing things that really matter and not be deceived into thinking that what may seem mundane and everyday doesn't matter for legacy purposes. God can use every single one of us to be a part of something so much bigger than ourselves: to be a light to those around us, pointing them to the living God of all the universe through seemingly simple things. We mustn't let our daily opportunities to influence others for eternity pass us by. I'm a daughter, a wife, a mother, a sister, an aunt, a friend, and a child of the King of Kings. I have a legacy I want to pass on to those who come behind me.

And I (Lauren) am still early in life, trying to think about stewarding the years I have ahead of me. I went against the trend of my millennial generation and got married young, while still in college. I met my husband, Michael, when we were both just seven years old. We started as Sunday school sweethearts, grew up in the same church, married in 2009 as twenty-one-year-old college students, and finished our last year of school together. Now we've embarked on the adventure of building our careers and dreaming about the future. Along the way, we've finished graduate degrees and are both now pursuing PhDs.

Just as I was finishing my undergraduate degree, I had the privilege of being the first person hired to work with the newly formed Museum of the Bible. During those early years, I experienced firsthand the rapid growth of a start-up project which turned into a world-class museum in Washington, D.C., less than eight years after its inception. Along the way, I remembered my passion for working in the corporate environment, and I recently transitioned into a role at Hobby Lobby, where I work as corporate ambassador.

In this journey, my husband and I have experienced the normal challenges of budgeting, the difficult seasons of marriage, the ache of infertility, and the challenge of having grace for each other. It is a story I hadn't quite expected, but as God reveals each step, I want to be intentional with the opportunities and challenges ahead of me.

We are people—women—just like you. Trying our best to spend our time on this earth in a way that makes a difference. Trying, succeeding, and stumbling along the way, trusting that even the mundane moments matter in an eternal scope. That is the hope for a legacy: to outlive our lives by the impact we leave behind.

Now, whenever the subject of legacy arises among Christians, it is usually a reference to the legacy of men. It's pretty safe to say that there are more men mentioned in the Bible, recognized throughout history, and likely to be recognized in leadership roles even today, not just in our country but around the globe.

Does this mean that women don't matter as much? Of course not! We simply are more likely to be valued for roles that don't get a plaque or an award. This sentiment was reiterated by Bishop Ndimbe of Kenya when he said, "Train a man, you train an individual; train a woman, you build a nation." Not always, but most often, it is the women who have a directional and influential role in the way a society goes, because they are the ones most often taking care of that society's most valuable asset: the next generation.

As a woman, whether or not you happen to be a mother, you have an irreplaceable role in our society. God created women with unique gifts and traits, and we all have an important role in passing on our legacy of faith.

A classic illustration of legacy tracks the family lines of two colonial-era men—Jonathan Edwards and Max Juke. Perhaps you've seen or heard this illustration. Edwards, a Massachusetts Puritan revivalist and theologian, died in 1758. Juke, an irreligious and hard-drinking man, farmed and did manual labor jobs off and on in rural New York at roughly the same time. Both men fathered many children and thus produced a multitude of descendants.

More than one hundred years later, a sociologist by the name of Richard Dugdale carried out a remarkably detailed study of Juke's hundreds of descendants.[3] The study revealed a legacy largely of heartache, misery, criminality, imprisonment, alcoholism, and premature death. Clearly, not all legacies are positive ones. Nevertheless, this remarkable research prompted another researcher to perform a similar exercise with the offspring of Jonathan Edwards.[4] By 1900, among the preacher's more than fourteen hundred descendants, the researcher discovered:

- Three hundred preachers
- One hundred missionaries
- Eighty public office holders (including one vice president of the United States and thirteen US senators)
- Seventy-five military officers
- Thirteen college presidents
- Many doctors, lawyers, and teachers

Two men. Two legacies.

But what about the legacy of women? The legacy of Jonathan Edwards belongs equally to his wife of more than thirty years, Sarah (Pierpont) Edwards. These are *her* descendants too. Some biographers and historians have suggested that Jonathan Edwards' impact and prominence never would have materialized apart from his partnership with Sarah. She was a remarkable

Christian woman who contributed equally to her family's legacy, even if it was not from the pulpit or the stage.

For too long we've thought of legacy-leaving as primarily the concern of men. Countless bronze monuments in American parks and town squares stand as silent reminders of the exploits or achievements of our manly generals, inventors, and founders. Of course, it is right that these leaders are honored so. We are all the beneficiaries of their courage, perseverance, and genius. But few women are honored for their leadership on the battlefield or in the corporate boardroom. And there are forms of leadership that go beyond these realms and are just as important. Profound and lasting legacies are often forged in quieter, less visible ways. Sarah Edwards is only one of these amazing women of legacy who lived her one life for Christ with remarkable faithfulness.

In these pages, we plan to reveal the underappreciated truth that Christian women can and do lead, and that history is filled with examples of bold, courageous, innovative women who loved God and rose to face the challenge of their times, forging a lasting impact on the course of human events. In every respect, these women were just like you and us. At the same time, they clearly displayed specific virtues that we can all cultivate and emulate.

Through the stories and journeys of these women, as well as through some of our own journeys, and by examining twelve characteristics of women of legacy, we hope to be encouragers of *your* journey of legacy.

What Is Legacy?

So what do we mean by legacy? It's certainly a grand word, and a daunting word at that. So let's start by what we don't mean. Legacy is not the idea of leaving financial wealth to someone. It's not reserved only for people whose names will be in history books, on monuments, or in record books. Legacy is far more. It is the story of your life that lives on after you leave this earth. You write this story every day through the values you embrace and live out. Your legacy can be positive or destructive, but the outcome is always up to you. When viewed from this lens of small daily actions and how they add up, creating a legacy is the most important job we can undertake.

Even God's design of the human body testifies to this feminine capacity for legacy. Geneticists tell us that every living person has a special form of DNA housed in every cell of his or her body, residing inside microscopic structures called mitochondria. This mitochondrial DNA is passed down only from our mothers. Your mother received hers from her mother. And she from her mother, and so forth, reaching back through the maternal generations into the ancient mists of human history to mankind's first mother. Every living person on earth is a product of this amazing maternal legacy.

In a similar way, there are certain cultural and societal impacts that we women are uniquely gifted by God to make. In every place on earth and in every time in history, right down to ours, women have been the keepers of the flame of family unity and the binders of the cords of connectedness. We are seemingly handcrafted by God Himself to be the conversation starters, the communication hubs, and the culture keepers.

Typically, women serve as the family scribes and historians. With our scrapbooks, newsletters, cards, and social media posts, we celebrate the milestones, keep in touch with friends and family members, share the news of both victories and challenges, and chronicle every aspect of family history. Who lovingly fills out the baby books and family Bibles? We do.

We also tend to function as the cultivators of connection and relationship. Who organizes the holiday gatherings and family reunions? Who plans the office Christmas celebrations and birthday parties? Who reaches out consistently to distant loved ones to keep the bonds of relationship mended and strong? Who gets teased about the amount of time spent on the phone or on social media, making sure everyone feels heard and valued and loved? In most cases, it is we women.

We are usually the ones reading the stories or saying the bedtime prayers, snuggling in rocking chairs, whispering words of comfort, affirmation, and biblical truth into impressionable little ears. It is at our knees where those little ones are likely to first hear about the love of a mighty yet kind Father and about the gentle Shepherd who loves and cares for His sheep.

It is in our nature to pour ourselves into the ones we love, and that is a beautiful part of legacy. Legacy is so much more than your family history or the possessions you pass on to the next generation. As Dr. James Dobson once said at a conference, "Heritage is what you *give* to someone. Legacy is what you do *in* someone."

All of this and more endows the Christian woman with an amazing power, not to mention an immense responsibility. Our unique roles and gifts provide us with the opportunity to be *influencers*. How we use that power is up to us. We can wield it in positive, negative, or neutral ways.

You see, God has designated a pathway for women that, when followed, leads to a significant, positive impact that extends beyond our days and expands for generations. Author Max Lucado calls this "outliving your life."[5] Others might call it creating a godly legacy. Whatever you call it, this influence is vital. You are uniquely created and equipped to become a woman of legacy. Are you ready to start building?

The Pathway to Becoming Women of Legacy

We believe God has marked a pathway for becoming the women of legacy our times so desperately need. The good news is, we have three wonderful sources for wisdom and insight on how to walk this path.

First and foremost, we have the Word of God. All of Scripture is important, but the lives of certain women of the Bible are a particularly rich source of inspiration.

Second, we have the inspiring examples of Christian women throughout history who rose to the challenges of their times, answered the call to leadership, and in doing so, established a powerful legacy. Some can accurately be said to have changed the course of history. Some are household names, but many did their leading and legacy building in quiet obscurity.

Third, we have shining examples among us today. There are women all over the world living out their faith in a multitude of significant ways.

As we go along, we'll share the journey of these ordinary women who have believed. By highlighting these women, we are not suggesting that they are perfect. The truth is, we are all flawed people whom God is transforming and healing. As a result, we wrestled with how to share the stories of these modern-day legacy builders whose stories are still being written. Any one of us might stumble at some point in the future. Yet we are mindful that through the cross of Christ, there is grace for all of us, and we all need it in equal measure.

Any future failings wouldn't invalidate the inspiring truth of the examples these women are providing today. So we will highlight the diversity of ways God can and does use us women when we submit to His wonderful, infallible Word and follow His Son, our Savior. Although each generation of women from the beginning of time has faced challenges, we feel now more than ever the need to encourage women of faith to realize the potential impact they can have. We are surrounded by a culture that is heavily influenced by social media and the entertainment world, which most often doesn't resonate with our foundational beliefs. It is important to remember what really matters and why we believe what we believe, and to keep that at the forefront of each day.

In the following chapters, we'll bring all three types of women forward as witnesses to testify, to teach, and to inspire. And we'll offer some thoughts about how their powerful stories can impact a woman today. By the time we're done, we believe, you'll be better equipped—and encouraged—to be the woman of legacy God has called you to be.

Like Marie Green, and like so many other women who have gone before us, you have only one life. It is an extraordinary gift from God. Let's learn to use our precious days on earth to make an impact that will last. No matter who you are, no matter what qualifications you feel you have or don't have, we all have a few things in common: we have twenty-four hours in a day, and we have a desire for God to use our lives for His glory. That's more than enough! So let's be women who get busy doing good with the time that we have.

CHAPTER 1

THE LEGACY OF COURAGE

The uplift of a fearless heart will help us over barriers. No one ever overcomes difficulties by going at them in a hesitant, doubtful way.

—Laura Ingalls Wilder

Y ou know, sometimes all you need is twenty seconds of insane courage." That's how Barbara Green, quoting Benjamin Mee of *We Bought a Zoo*, likes to start some of her speeches when sharing about her journey all the way to the Supreme Court of the United States in the *Burwell v. Hobby Lobby* case. When we think of courage, we tend to think of men on a battlefield in some heroic fight. But women? Oh, we have courage too.

It's so true: all it takes is twenty seconds of insane courage. Courage often comes in the everyday, the common, the unrecognized. Sometimes it is simply courage to face the day, the crying baby, the distant husband, or the circumstances of your everyday life. Take a peek with us.

The Courage of the Outcast

Esther—or Hadassah, as she was known as a little girl—gingerly places the ornate golden wine goblet at the king's designated place at the table. She eyes it for a moment, then turns it a few degrees so the royal seal faces precisely forward. As she and her handmaidens meticulously lay out the banquet table, the young queen of Persia can't help but think of a verse from one of the ancient songs of her people. More than five centuries before her time, long before this seemingly endless era of captivity and exile, a future king of Israel had sung: "You prepare a table before me in the presence of my enemies."

On this night, it is Esther who prepares a table for two invited guests. The first is her husband, King Ahasuerus, known to the Greeks as Xerxes of Persia, the god-emperor of the largest empire the world has yet seen. The other is her enemy—a wicked, powerful government official who burns with an unholy, murderous hatred for all her people. This is a man who has the king's ear and his trust, one of the most well-connected men in all the empire.

Tonight Esther, the orphan girl who came to the palace out of obscurity, is going to accuse him face-to-face of treason.

Doing so, however, requires that she also reveal to the king her most explosive secret. She has deceived him, or at least she has withheld the whole truth about herself. That truth? She is but one of the tens of thousands of Jewish exiles living in the Persian Empire. *She is an outcast.* She doesn't belong in the palace of the king.

She cannot guess how he will react to this revelation, but she is terrifyingly aware of his reputation for fits of wild, irrational rage. She knows he once commanded that the sea be punished with three hundred lashes after a sudden storm destroyed a temporary bridge he'd just constructed across the narrow strait dividing his empire from Greece.

Yes, the man who'd once sought to have the ocean itself whipped into submission is about to hear from her own lips that she isn't who he thinks she is. So to calm her racing mind and heart, she quietly sings a song of her people:

Even though I walk through the valley of the shadow
of death,
 I will fear no evil,
for you are with me;
 your rod and your staff,
 they comfort me.

The biblical story of Esther is a majestic story, but within that story there is a simple truth. Esther doesn't belong. She is not of royal descent. She is no princess, let alone a queen—at least that's what the voices inside her head are telling her. Worse still, she's Jewish. She's an exile. She's living away from her homeland. She's an orphan. Her parents are gone, and she was taken in and raised by her cousin.

Somehow, with all these strikes against her, she's become the queen to a man she doesn't love. The fine clothes she wears, the perfume, the attendants to wait on her every need are finery that she considers foreign. Every day her heart cries out in wonder, *What am I doing here?* And in the same breath, *I don't belong.*

We suspect that the voices inside Esther's head are the voices you've heard as well. They are all the voices telling you that you don't belong or aren't good enough or don't measure up to some magazine or television ad.

The saga for Esther doesn't end, however, simply with her elevation to the position of queen. There's something more. It seems that God always has something more for us, something that might stretch us well beyond what we might choose for ourselves. Her people are in peril. They will certainly suffer and die at the edict of the king. Her cousin approaches her and asks her to do the unthinkable: speak to the king on behalf of her people.

Her heart has a thousand objections. You can hear them: *I'm not a speaker. I'm just a young girl. No one can approach the king without permission.* And perhaps the darkest thought: *I'll have to reveal my true identity.*

Her cousin is insistent. People will die unless she acts. Even though she never chose her position, it was given to her. Surely, it is "for such a time as this." So perhaps today you can imagine with me this young girl queen making all of her preparations— the prayers, the fasting, the counsel—but still it comes down to this one moment. Outside the king's chambers, her feet scuffle on the palace floor, and her heart catches in her throat. And twenty seconds of insane courage seize the outcast girl as she enters the forbidden room for permission to speak. Those twenty seconds will change the course of her people's fate.

THE COURAGE TO SPEAK

We are all like Esther. In so many ways, the world tells us that we don't belong and that we don't fit. Truly, we are exiles and outcasts. This world is not our home, and we all have our fears. I (Jackie) have long struggled with some of these ideas.

I didn't go to college. I became a wife at eighteen and a mother at twenty. For most of my adult life, I've been immersed in the day-to-day world of the supposed mundane—the cooking, the cleaning, the kids. But when my husband began pursuing the vision of building the Museum of the Bible, a massive, 430,000-square-foot museum in the heart of Washington, D.C., I was pulled into the spotlight with him. Through the project, Steve and I have received far more media attention and public scrutiny in one year than in all the previous years of our life. I helped organize women's events, decorate, design gifts, choose menus, and do whatever was needed in the development years leading up to the opening. I was called on to represent the museum and to seek support for the museum efforts. For the first time in my life, I found myself up on stage speaking to hundreds, even thousands, of people.

I found my own heart crying out, *I'm not a speaker; I'm just a mom!* So that's what I talked about—being a mom, waiting in the school carpool line, helping kids with nightly homework, mentoring adult children, and letting the Bible impact my everyday life. As I told my story, God slowly began removing my fears of the stage. Like Esther, I found my voice. As I shared my own experiences, I found that women from all walks of life were coming up to me and wanting to talk. They identified with me—being called to a place where I wasn't comfortable and for which I didn't feel equipped. And they too yearned, as I did, to make a difference no matter what the stage would be.

So what about your setting? What situation have you been placed in "for such a time as this"? I've always heard it said that courage is about ordinary people doing extraordinary things, and maybe that's a good place for all of us to start.

Maybe your courage shows up as you see an injustice, and instead of being an observer, you choose to speak up. Maybe it shows up as you raise a child with disabilities or emotional trauma. Or when you face illness of your own or of a family member. Maybe it comes as you persevere through a troubled marriage. Perhaps it is being a single mom with kids to raise and bills to pay. Maybe your courage shows up as you embrace healthy vulnerability and share about a personal struggle, inviting others into your life and showing them they aren't alone. It could simply be the courage to exercise faith in making your family's budget work. Every one of us has to pull our courage out to overcome fears that assail us regarding challenges like these and many others.

Whatever the situation, each of us has been providentially placed in a unique set of circumstances. The situation in which God has placed you may not look anything like ours. In fact, it almost certainly won't. The apostle Paul said, "*I* run the race set before *me*," indicating that we each have our own God-ordained race to run. We can't know your individual situation. What is certain is that as a daughter of the King, you have a key role to play in the context within which God has set you.

You are called and commissioned to lead, to exert influence in the lives of others. And stepping into that role will, without a doubt, bring you to moments that require more courage than you think you possess.

Of course, courage doesn't mean not experiencing fear. No, it means that we, as Dr. Susan Jeffers once wrote, "feel the fear and do it anyway."[1] We don't banish fear; we overcome it by acting in spite of it. This is what author Holly Wagner calls "finding your brave": "We don't just find our brave and survive the storms for ourselves. God designed us to live in community so that our experiences can help others. People all around us are looking for help as they navigate the challenges, and we can demonstrate a victorious way of living, even in challenging times."[2]

As Holly points out, we don't press through our fears only for ourselves and our personal victories. As in Esther's story, the fates of other people hang in the balance. Often it's our loved ones who are counting on us. Women of legacy understand that our victories can and do impact countless others as well, including generations yet to be born.

The annals of church history are filled with women who pressed through their fears and found the courage to follow God's call. In extreme circumstances, that call requires a willingness to risk death or torture for the cause of Christ. Women believers in the Middle East and in other hot spots around the world face this as a daily reality. For most of us, however, the need for courage arises in less dramatic but no less important ways.

THE COURAGE TO TRY

For me (Lauren), pushing back fear seems far less dramatic, especially when I compare the small challenges in my life with other women's harder battles. But that is the problem with comparing, isn't it? No one wins. This is a problem particularly felt among women. When we live our lives out of decisions based on comparing ourselves with others, we are not living in the fullness of what God has for us.

Two years ago, a dear friend of mine pushed back her fears and moved halfway across the world to settle into a new home in North Africa. She knew she was called, and I was amazed to watch her courage as she packed up her life, leaving the comforts that are offered here, and moved to a place where less than 1 percent of the population believes in the same God she does. Ruth (name changed for security) is eager to serve the people in her new context, and she is finding joy from walking in courage.

When I consider that example of courage from someone so close, I can feel small. But we must be reminded that God calls each of us to a different journey, and that requires us to be in tune with the Holy Spirit's leading. Then it takes courage to take that first step in obedience!

For me, that's meant pursuing a PhD in ethics and public policy. I have always loved learning. I love the whole process of reading, thinking, and writing. Some of that love of learning is evidenced by my pursuit and completion of two master's degrees. When I heard about this unique program, I was intrigued by the way this program brought together my interests in theology and the public square. I wanted to be challenged to think deeply about how Christians can live out a thoughtful public theology. But pursuing a PhD was a tall mountain. No one in our family had ever pursued such an advanced degree. I had a lot of fears in going farther. My fears were different from Ruth's, but they were felt fears. I wondered whether I was up for the intellectual challenge, whether I could keep up with my fellow students, and whether I would compare favorably with my peers. My biggest fear was of failure. What if I couldn't handle the languages that are required to get into a PhD program? What if I couldn't keep up with people who had a scholarly, academic mind? There were a thousand what ifs, all rooted in fear.

I had felt for years this was something God was putting in my heart. It took time, but eventually I decided I had to try. And that's what I'm learning—the courage to try.

The Courage to Be Alone

If there's any detriment to courage, it has to be the sense of being alone.

In 1988, workers sifting through the rubble of what had once been the historic Tengchow Christian Church in Penglai, China, discovered something remarkable buried in the debris. Beneath the chunks of brick and plaster, they found a toppled stone memorial slab engraved in Chinese characters, featuring the name of an American woman who died in 1912.

The name lovingly engraved on the monument was that of Charlotte Moon—known to the world as "Lottie."

The crushing weight of Communist persecution under the dictator Mao Tse-tung had forced the members of the once-vibrant church underground in the 1950s. The abandoned church building fell into disrepair and ultimately collapsed. But as repression by the Chinese government eased in the late 1980s, the church's members surfaced and began to restore and rebuild with the help of American donors. That is how the construction workers came to find the stone tribute to the living legacy of Lottie Moon.

This tiny, four-foot-three-inch woman left a legacy of immense depth and breadth. Hundreds of churches across China can trace their spiritual roots back to the work of Lottie Moon. She inspired hundreds of other missionaries and rallied funding for their work. It is no exaggeration to say that millions of Chinese believers, past and present, can attribute their citizenship in the kingdom of God to the courageous work of this one bold, little lady.

Born to a wealthy Virginia family, she was well educated in an era in which this was uncommon. Moon earned one of the first master's degrees ever awarded to a woman in the American South. A fellow educator called her the "most cultivated woman" he had ever known. Lottie was living a comfortable life filled with meaningful work, running schools for girls, when suddenly she heard—"clear as a bell," in her words—God's call to serve in China.

So in 1873, Lottie, thirty-three years of age and single, stepped *alone* onto a steamship bound for China. When she docked on a Shandong Province pier in the coastal city now known as Penglai, she found herself surrounded by eighty thousand souls who had never heard of Jesus.

Despite her apparent deficits—being small in size and having no accompanying partner—Lottie Moon had a simple yet bold strategy. She planned to leverage her experience in running schools for girls into a strategy for evangelizing and educating women and girls. In 1873's China, this was simply unheard of and certainly frowned upon. She knew, however, that winning the women was the key to reaching the children and thereby the next generation of Chinese.

By 1878, Moon had immersed herself in the study of the language and then launched a boarding school for young girls, the first of many such schools she eventually established for Chinese girls and boys. Initially, the locals viewed her work with a mix of suspicion and open hostility. Eventually, however, her genuine love for the people and her servant's heart won them over.

As her work expanded and gathered momentum, Moon began writing to churches and publications back in the United States, urging support for the missions work there and elsewhere. She also encouraged her fellow Southern Baptists to expand the role of, and expand opportunities for, women in missions.

Roughly ten years after her arrival, firmly established in her coastal Chinese home and fluent in the language, Lottie once again felt the pull of God's call into the unknown. Leaving behind the familiarity and safety of her adopted home, she threw herself into what she called her "country work."

In the years that followed, she traveled tirelessly, criss-crossing an inland area of China more than ten thousand miles square. Keep in mind, this is rural imperial China in the 1880s! Everywhere Lottie traveled, she shared the gospel. Where did she find the courage for this kind of life? In a letter to the mission board back home, she once wrote, "As you wend your way from village to village, you feel it is no idle fancy that the Master walks beside you and you hear his voice saying gently, 'Lo! I am with you always even unto the end.'"[3]

China's men also hungered to be taught about the Jesus she boldly proclaimed. On one occasion, a delegation of men from Pingdu, more than three hundred miles away, walked that distance to plead with her to come "teach truth" in their city.

Moon heeded their call, riding a mule for four days to reach the inland city and making her home there for the next seven years. She rented a tiny house with a dirt floor, living and dressing exactly as her neighbors did. Lottie Moon is believed to be the first female foreign missionary to live alone among the Chinese people. In fact, she was the only non-Chinese person living in the entire city.

Across nearly forty years of extraordinary ministry in China, Lottie Moon impacted countless people and changed innumerable eternal destinies. She took only two brief furloughs in that span. Yet the most significant and enduring part of her legacy began with a single letter—one that challenged other women to become women of legacy.

While living and working in Pingdu, Lottie penned a letter to the *Foreign Mission Journal,* a publication of the Southern Baptist Convention in the US, challenging Baptist women to rise to a greater level of energy and involvement in funding missionary work. In a shrewd but gentle rebuke, she pointed admiringly to the efforts of Methodist women and wondered out loud why her Baptist sisters seemed either unwilling or unable to do as much to reach the world for Jesus. "They give freely and cheerfully. Now the painful question arises. 'What is the matter, that we Baptists give so little? Whose is the fault? Is it a fact that our women are lacking in the enthusiasm, the organizing power, and the executive ability that so conspicuously distinguishes our Methodist sisters?'"[4]

She went on to suggest an annual Christmas season of prayer and offerings for missions. The letter succeeded beyond her wildest hopes. Congregations all over the country took up Lottie's challenge, giving birth to what ultimately became the yearly Lottie Moon Christmas Offering.

In its first year, the campaign raised more than $3,300 and funded three additional women missionaries for Lottie's expanding efforts in China. The campaign grew rapidly each year thereafter. Today the fund that carries her name raises roughly $150 million each year for missionary activity around the world. To date, Lottie's little letter of challenge has resulted in more than $1 billion in offerings in support of global evangelism.[5] You read that correctly. That's billion with a *b.*

Throughout her life as a missionary in China, Lottie Moon stood just barely above four feet tall. At death, she weighed about fifty pounds, her body ravaged by illness and hardship. Nevertheless, this tiny woman made a gigantic impact in her generation, an impact that is still expanding today. She was a woman of legacy who conquered her sense of being alone by leaning on a God who says, "I am with you always."

Your unique call might not demand a harrowing journey to a faraway place, but it will almost certainly stretch you. Running the race God sets before you may not require immersing yourself in an alien culture, but it will undoubtedly pull you out of your comfort zone. Anyone who dares to step out in an effort to exert positive, godly influence in this fallen, twisted world is sure to encounter trouble, persecution, or both. That positive, godly influence may flow from something as simple as interacting with the people placed in your path (such as a cashier at the grocery store), teaching a class at your church, hosting a Bible study or prayer group in your home, serving on boards in your community, interfacing with coworkers, taking on leadership roles in your career, or just making the day-to-day effort of molding a meaningful life.

Yet here's the wonder of courage. Sometimes, as with Lottie Moon, all it takes is a simple letter. Or perhaps the response to a nudge that really doesn't make sense. All along the way, God gives the strength, and He makes it possible. Make no mistake, there will be doubts and storms along the way, but the value of legacy is counted at the *end* of the journey. We have no idea where the path will take us, but we can't be paralyzed by the not knowing. We need only take the next step, even if it seems we are alone.

The Courage of the Broken

When we think of legacy and courage, we tend to think of the strong, the capable. But rarely do we think of the broken.

Consider Joni Eareckson Tada. Most American believers have some familiarity with her story. She was seventeen in 1967 when a diving accident left her paralyzed from the shoulders down. Her bestselling 1976 book *Joni* chronicled her hard-fought victory over depression and doubt. That book ultimately became a feature-length film in which Joni played herself.

Despite the paralysis and the problems surrounding it, Joni went on to become an accomplished recording artist, painter, author, and speaker. More important, she became God's encouraging ambassador of faith to people with disabilities all over the world. In 1979, she founded Joni and Friends, an organization for Christian ministry in the disabled community throughout the world. In 2006, she broadened her capacity for long-term impact with the establishment of the Joni and Friends International Disability Center in Agoura, California.

Joni is the author of more than forty-eight books, and her daily four-minute radio program is heard on thousands of broadcast outlets in North America and online around the world. Using every avenue at her disposal, Joni points others to hope and a better life in God. Her life exemplifies choosing service over self-pity, faith over fear, and the beauty of worship over bitterness.

All of this is far more than enough to establish Joni as an inspiring model for courage in the face of adversity. She long ago qualified for the Women of Legacy Hall of Fame. Nevertheless, 2010 brought her another challenge to test her faith and her strength of will.

In October of 2010—Breast Cancer Awareness Month, as it happens—Joni was found to have a large growth in her right breast and was diagnosed with stage III cancer.

Such news is a huge blow to absorb for any woman, but it seemed to carry an extra element of shock for Joni. She had come to believe that the enormous burden of her disability somehow exempted her from other health challenges. As she shared in a 2012 blog post, "My attention was always focused on my quadriplegia—forty-five years in a wheelchair saddled me with enough medical challenges without thinking of cancer too . . . it had been nine years since my last mammogram."[6]

In a 2013 interview, she admitted that her first thought on

hearing the news was to think of the home-going that has been the ever-present possibility since her accident. "Privately I've wondered, gee, Lord, is this cancer my ticket to heaven? Because I sure am tired of sitting in a wheelchair and my body is aching. And I'm so weary. Could this be my ticket to heaven?"[7]

A mastectomy was quickly scheduled. Her first visit with her oncologist afterward was sobering. The surgery revealed that the cancer had spread to some of her lymph nodes, and these had been removed as well. She learned she now faced months of the kind of chemotherapy that tends to make life hellish for otherwise strong individuals, let alone a woman with the challenges and frailties Joni overcomes each day.

Joni recalls that when her doctor stepped out of the room for a moment, she broke down the moment he closed the door. "I can't do this," she sobbed into the comforting arms of her husband, Ken. Over and over she cried, "It's too much, too overwhelming. I can't do it!"

Of course, this is a perfectly natural reaction. Nevertheless, she didn't stay stuck in despair. When the shock of the news subsided, she set about meeting this new challenge with the same faith and courage that had carried her farther in life than anyone ever dreamed possible. "It was the only time I cried. After that, I grabbed hold of a couple of Scriptures and began to move forward. Psalm 27, 'The LORD is my light and my salvation. Whom shall I fear?' And from Psalm 28, 'The LORD is my strength and my shield; my heart trusts in him, and I am helped.' From that day on, I rehearsed those Bible verses and, oh, was I encouraged."[8]

Joni pressed through two years of treatments and came through the other side stronger and with an additional cause to champion. She now makes breast cancer awareness and screening a part of her crowded life mission, providing encouragement and support to women facing the same battle. Today she's busier than ever. In May of 2017, she and the organization she leads marked the thirty-fifth anniversary of her *Joni and Friends* radio program.

How did she do it? "I decided to not let cancer overwhelm me," she says. "I decided to overwhelm cancer with a shoring up of an attitude that would trust God in the midst of this and not doubt Him."[9]

In a 2009 interview, Joni offered us all some hard-won wisdom for gathering courage in the face of a seemingly overwhelming problem or challenge. She said, "The Bible has a remedy, a prescription, a medicine for melancholy. We are to remember and remember and remember again the way God worked in the past. So that's what I do. That has been my practice when my pain and the darkness try to push me into a lonely corner. I talk of His deeds. Right out loud."[10]

It's true. There is something spiritually and emotionally powerful about reminding yourself of God's past deeds of might, faithfulness, and kindness, both in your life and in the lives of others. It calms apprehensions and puts fears to flight. It stirs our faith. Doing so also redirects our focus from problem to solution. When the goodness and power of our awesome God becomes our focal point, even the most formidable challenges shrink into insignificance. Big God, small enemies.

We can't overestimate the power of our thoughts. It's easy to see how outer actions impact others, but our inner lives, our thoughts, carry just as much weight. The words "only what's done for Christ will last" can imply action, but sometimes the most important thing we can do for Christ is to submit our thoughts to Him. King David wrote in Psalm 19:14, "May the words of my mouth and the meditation of my heart be pleasing to you, O LORD" (NLT). To God, our inner thoughts are just as important as our outer actions.

In psychology, this can be referred to as "self-talk." Self-talk is that internal dialogue we have with ourselves. When we begin to recognize what kind of self-talk we have going on in our heads, we can change the direction of the message. Self-talk can be negative or positive. When we direct ourselves to the promises that we know God has for us in Scripture, and we direct that self-talk to remind us of His faithfulness to us in the past, it is easier to renew our hope by focusing on our big God. When we change how we are processing things cognitively (self-talk), our behavior will often follow.

THE COURAGE TO OVERCOME

If we're going to lead and become women of legacy, we must learn to channel our inner Wonder Woman and punch fear in the nose. That's literally what a fifty-three-year-old woman in Australia's Northern Territory did a few years ago.

Margaret Rinybuma was watching her nineteen-year-old nephew launch a boat on a riverbank when suddenly a ten-foot-long saltwater crocodile lunged out of the water and grabbed the young man by the leg, pulling him toward deeper water. As she later told the *Northern Territory News*, without thinking she jumped in after her nephew, socked the croc on the nose with her fist, and shouted, "No! In the name of Jesus!" The startled crocodile instantly released her nephew, who escaped with only some muscle tissue damage to his lower leg.

This is the kind of righteously angry "mama bear" instinct that we must learn to summon if we're going to press through fear and into our callings. Like the crocodile, fear often rises up unexpectedly, threatening to take away what we hold dear. But we can stake our courage in Christ, who gives us strength to confront even our deepest fears.

So what kinds of fears are we likely to encounter as we step into new levels of impact?

The fears you face may not be as literally life-and-death as the ones confronted by Esther or Lottie Moon. You probably will not have to confront a crocodile in defense of a loved one. But you will almost certainly come face-to-face with one or more of these common fears:

- Fear of failure (insufficiency, humiliation)
- Fear of man (social rejection)
- Fear of loss (losing money, relationships, opportunity, prestige)
- Fear of making a mistake (embarrassment)
- Fear of the spotlight (being seen, imperfection)

Fears can take a multitude of shapes and forms. But they all emerge from the same source, and they aren't from God. The Enemy comes to "steal and kill and destroy" (John 10:10). One way the Enemy will do that is by crippling us with fear. But we know that fear is not from the Lord. "God has not given us a spirit of fear, but of power and of love and of a sound mind" (2 Tim. 1:7 NKJV).

Florence Nightingale, who laid the foundations for the modern nursing profession on the bloody battle lines of the Crimean War in the 1850s, once wrote, "How very little can be done under the spirit of fear."[11]

In a similar vein, Pastor Rick Warren has written, "Fear-driven people often miss great opportunities because they're afraid to venture out. . . . Fear is a self-imposed prison that will keep you from becoming what God intends for you to be. You must move against it with the weapons of faith and love."[12]

Courage is not so much about great marches into battle or life-changing decisions. Rather courage is most often found in the subtle, daily acts of recognizing opportunities beyond the challenges and stepping out in brave faith toward that reality. It's about taking the step—sometimes alone, often into the unknown—and allowing the Lord to use our brokenness. Those small steps add up to a lifetime lived courageously and the legacy that goes with it.

CHAPTER 2

THE LEGACY OF GENEROSITY

*Giving frees us from the familiar territory
of our own needs by opening our mind to the
unexplored worlds occupied by the needs of
others.*

—Barbara Bush[1]

It's funny how the simplest gifts leave a lasting impact. Marie Green wanted to give to missionaries above and beyond what she and her husband could give. So she crocheted doilies and sold them to give the funds to missions. She could not have realized the impact that those doilies would have on her son David, who watched her demonstrate faithfulness creatively with whatever means she had. Today those doilies still serve to influence David and Hobby Lobby to support the efforts of missions around the world.

Marie's story reminds us of another woman's simple gift. The Scriptures do not tell us her name, but they record her humble act of faith.

The Power of Generosity

Her day started out like most of her days. Quiet. Her meager fare consisted of hard-crusted bread. She was grateful for the little she had. Her eyes looked to the sky as she considered the Scripture "Give thanks to the LORD, for he is good; his love endures forever" (1 Chron. 16:34). The house was bare, with just some fragments of furniture; a small fire burned gently. She swept the house before she left, although it was already clean.

She made the trek daily to the temple. Although her worship was ever a fresh experience, the ritual was always the same. Prayers of thanksgiving. Prayers of praise. Prayers of supplication for others. And then she made her offering—her gift. It was her joy to give to the Lord.

Her purse was almost empty and her cupboards back home were bare, but her heart was full. She approached the treasury clutching her two coins, her last two coins. The line was steady. Others went before her, and some had gifts that made large clanging noises. The amounts were much bigger. For her, there was no shame in the size of her gift. When it was her turn, she simply let loose from her grasp two small coins and turned to leave.

On this day, there was a man watching. He saw her gift. He was surrounded by His disciples, and He sought to make a point with them. It would be easy to get lost in the finery and the show of giving, but this man, Jesus, taught His disciples that giving was never a question of the amount. It was instead always a matter of the heart. "'Truly I tell you,' he said, 'this poor widow has put in more than all the others. All these people gave their gifts out of their wealth; but she out of her poverty put in all she had to live on'" (Luke 21:3–4).

Two small coins. Of all the many gifts, big and small, that have ever been given, this gift, we suspect, is the most famous one. Today the gift of this nameless woman is called "the widow's mite." It is the symbol of generosity all around the world. This gift is so significant that Jesus used it as a teaching tool for His disciples.

What is the lesson of the widow's mite? How does this woman speak to us? Because she was a widow, her situation was likely destitute. She was at the low end of the economic and social scale. The disciples would have recognized this. She ignored the laws of good financial planning that said she should save her last pennies for a rainy day. She disregarded her own need and invested in a greater good—worship through giving.

She challenges us with a simple thought: Everyone can be generous. We all can give what's in our hand. Do you have money? Do you have time? Do you have a specific talent? These are all gifts that can be given.

Few traits carry as much power for creating a lasting legacy as generosity. The Scriptures are filled with promises and encouragement assuring us that being a giver brings joy and impact in this life as well as great reward.

We have personally observed the legacy-building power of a lifestyle of generosity. Marie Green passed down a legacy of generosity to her son David, our father-in-law and grandfather respectively. We gather routinely as a family to discuss our giving opportunities. A committee reviews and makes decisions on giving corporately, viewing each request through a specific lens: Will it advance God's Word? Will it save a person's soul?

The impact of this family generosity is now being carried on to a third generation. Four times a year, David's grandchildren get together to consider requests that they examine and decide whether to support. This allows the third generation to practice generosity themselves. I (Lauren) get to participate actively in these quarterly meetings, and I'm looking forward to the day when the fourth generation will get to join in these meetings as well.

On top of these giving activities, our family also meets once a year to revisit our vision and mission statements. This celebration gives us time to connect on the essential values that bind us all together. It allows us time to recognize and celebrate the ways we have been able to carry out our legacy as a family each year. A little woman named Marie greatly influenced these efforts.

This spiritual ethic runs deep. In his 2017 book *Giving It All Away . . . and Getting It All Back Again: The Way of Living Generously*, David writes, "My journey into generosity has shown me two important things, among others. First, generosity has a starting point. You don't just wake up one day and *poof*, you're generous. It begins with a decision to steward your resources with a heavenly mindset. Second, generosity depends not on how much money we have but on the posture of our hearts. Too often we think of generosity as the sharing and giving of money. But that's a shallow definition. Generosity goes much deeper."[2]

Generosity can show itself through time, talents, and treasure. David reminds us that while his mother, Marie, had very little in terms of financial resources, she was exceedingly generous with her faith, her talents, and the little money that she did have. We can all be generous—with our time, our energies, our actions, our words—no matter how much money we have. Generosity, as a way of life, stands in sharp contrast to the way of the world. Although greed and selfishness have reigned throughout most of human history, the gospel proves more powerful, since wherever the gospel of Jesus Christ has spread, human hearts have been softened and bent toward generosity and concern for others.

I (Jackie) often hear generosity encouraged, but it can be easy to make excuses, like being too busy, and not participate. Generosity toward people who are less fortunate is taught throughout the Bible. Specifically, I think of these verses regarding generosity:

- "Remembering the words the Lord Jesus himself said: 'It is more blessed to give than to receive'" (Acts 20:35).
- "Generous hands are blessed hands because they give bread to the poor" (Prov. 22:9 MSG).
- "Whoever is kind to the poor lends to the Lord, and he will reward them for what they have done" (Prov. 19:17).

- "A gift opens the way and ushers the giver into the presence of the great" (Prov. 18:16).
- "Do to others as you would have them do to you" (Luke 6:31).

If life is all about me, then it won't take long to get bored. We need more than self-satisfaction and greediness to be truly content. If all we did was store up treasures on this earth, I believe, we would all get to the end of our lives feeling quite a lot of despair. What good would it do? You may have heard the saying "You'll never see a hearse pulling a U-Haul." We can't take the treasures with us when our lives on earth are over. So why not invest in things that last?

Unfortunately, the question of living generously does not come up often enough. Yet generosity is the only known antidote to greed. Here's a question: Are we willing to challenge ourselves—right now—to give our possessions and our financial resources to relieve the suffering of others? That question is illustrated by the story of a little-known princess born to privilege in medieval Europe.

The Sacrifice of Generosity

What would you do if your world teetered on the brink of collapse? Would you draw everything tight and seek security? Or would you live and give recklessly?

SEEING THE SUFFERING

Elizabeth looks down from the window of her Danube River fortress in the forested heart of Europe and scans the pitiful sea of desperate people huddled at the gates and around the walls. There are hundreds, perhaps thousands, of them, and more are arriving each week.

She is barely nineteen years old but she is their queen, and a sudden famine has plunged her land—a Germanic domain called Thuringia—into deep crisis. Her beloved husband, the king, might know what to do. However, young Ludwig IV, Landgrave of Thuringia, is half a world away, fighting in the Holy Land.

Something must be done, and quickly. A peasant uprising could overthrow the monarchy. Elizabeth knows that other European monarchs have already lost their kingdoms while away fighting Islamic Saracens in the land of the Bible. Even so, it is not fear of the mob that moves Elizabeth. It is a heart of compassion. The teenaged princess has already developed a reputation among her people for kindness and service to the poorest of the poor in her land. This is why the starving now come to the doorstep of the Hungarian princess. Anger doesn't drive them. Hope does.

A STORY NOT OF HER OWN MAKING

Elizabeth of Hungary was born in 1207 at the royal castle of Pozsony, in what is today Bratislava, Slovakia. Her father was King Andrew II of Hungary. Both sides of her family tree were filled with central and eastern European royalty stretching back for centuries. Elizabeth inherited a fierce Christian faith from her mother, Gertrude.

Elizabeth was only four years old when she was betrothed to young prince Ludwig of Thuringia. This future union was crafted to strengthen political alliances between kingdoms. To that end, her parents sent her to live in the Thuringian court while she was still very small, to learn the German language and customs. When she was only seven, Elizabeth received word that her mother had been assassinated in an act of palace intrigue.

Elizabeth resolved not to let her circumstances bring her down. She showed early on a deep love for God and for common people. Her future in-laws began to wonder if this little girl was a little *too* spiritual and holy to make a suitable mate for their son, the prince. As the children grew, they began to contemplate calling the union off, but Ludwig wouldn't hear of it. He shared his future bride's zealous faith and admired her concern for the poor.

When Elizabeth was only fourteen and Ludwig nineteen, the long-awaited marriage was transacted. That very year, Ludwig's father died, and Ludwig took the throne of Thuringia. He did so in a time of economic crisis and political turmoil in the land.

The young queen brought enormous wealth to the union. Her dowry included five castles and estates in Hungary. This had earned her the early nickname Elizabeth of Many Castles. Yet the teen monarch immediately embarked on efforts to use that wealth to help the destitute and suffering. Exposure to the new writings of a young Italian friar by the name of Francis of Assisi further stoked her passion for benevolence. Within those writings, she came across this declaration: "Remember that when you leave this earth, you can take with you nothing you have received, fading symbols of honor, trappings of power, but only what you have given: a full heart enriched by honest service, love, sacrifice, and courage."

With all of her great wealth, Elizabeth had a decision to make: What would she do with what she had been given?

Taking to heart the words of Francis of Assisi, she quickly acted to aid others. She became a patroness of Francis's new monastic order, the Franciscans, and helped establish a monastery in Thuringia. She also used her dowry to found eastern Europe's first orphanage. She established houses for the care of lepers and with her own hands got personally involved in even the most unpleasant parts of their care. Her husband's family was appalled and scandalized by the young queen's insistence on wading into the muck and misery of her most pitiful subjects.

A FURTHER TEST OF GENEROSITY

Then came the famine of 1226. There was widespread starvation, followed by outbreaks of crime and disease. Reports reached Elizabeth that many of her subjects were grinding up pine bark as a substitute for flour simply to get something into their empty stomachs. The situation grew grimmer by the day.

With a desperate mob pressing against the castle gates, her advisors urged her to call out the military to disperse the crowd. Elizabeth prayed for wisdom and gave a very different order.

She ordered the royal family's personal reserves of food distributed to the crowd. She also commanded that the castle's bread ovens operate day and night and that the bread be distributed as widely as possible. She then enlisted the aid of numerous monasteries, convents, and abbeys she had long supported. Soup kitchens operated by monks and nuns sprang up overnight across the country. At Elizabeth's urging, church doors throughout the land were thrown open to the homeless. Firewood was distributed to people who were too weak to gather it for themselves.

Still, Elizabeth went farther. Her husband's relatives looked on in helpless outrage as she took all the ready money in the royal treasury and had it distributed among the sick and starving. She began with her own personal jewels, selling even the treasured silver cradle that held her as an infant princess of Hungary.

These actions exhausted the royal wealth but won the hearts and undying loyalty of the common people. It was clear to the nation that Elizabeth did everything in her power to ease suffering and save lives in a time of national emergency.

As Ludwig returned home, messengers dispatched by his relatives met him at a distance. They breathlessly and scornfully related the news of how his overly spiritual wife had bankrupted the royal family in her foolish efforts to feed peasants. Yet Ludwig did not respond with the anger they expected. Instead he asked,

"Do I still have all my domains?" The answer, of course, was yes. His bride's swift actions had quelled any possibility of an uprising and preserved his throne. He was more secure than ever because of the people's gratitude.

The couple, very much in love and united in devotion to God, seemed poised to live happily ever after. Yet this was not to be. A year later, Ludwig departed for the Holy Land to lead what would ultimately be called the Sixth Crusade. He contracted the plague while en route and died before ever reaching Jerusalem. Ludwig's brother then assumed the throne. Grief-stricken, Elizabeth entered monastic life and became a third-order Franciscan, following in the footsteps of her inspiration and role model, Saint Francis of Assisi.

From that point forward, Elizabeth traded the fabulous, ornate dresses of her youth for the simple gray robe of a Franciscan. Rather than being waited on by attendants, she washed lepers with her own hands. She worked wool and operated a loom like any peasant girl. She fell ill and died only four years after the death of her husband.

Elizabeth of Hungary is venerated by Roman Catholics, Anglicans, and Lutherans around the world today as Saint Elizabeth of Thuringia. She married at fourteen, was widowed at twenty, and died at twenty-four. Yet in only ten eventful years she became a woman of extraordinary legacy through the power of generosity.

The widow's mite. Saint Elizabeth. On the one hand, they seem vastly different. Great poverty versus great wealth. Yet the similarity of these women is striking. Both the widow and Saint Elizabeth responded to their circumstances by giving generously. And their generosity impacted generations.

It seems that the widow and Elizabeth ask a basic question: What do you see? An empty purse or an opportunity to worship? A castle under siege, or hungry and hurting people? So often our prayer needs to be, "O God, change my eyesight!" And with changed eyesight, perhaps we can even multiply our generosity many times over.

The Power of Multiplying Generosity

Mary Beth Chapman. Most of you may know her singer-songwriter husband, Steven Curtis Chapman. For years, she was content to be the anchor of their family in Nashville with their three children while her husband piled up numerous bestselling music albums and toured continuously, ministering to people across the globe. However, something happened in 1997 that would change all of that.

That year, Mary Beth and her eleven-year-old daughter Emily traveled with some friends to Haiti for a mission trip hosted by Compassion International. The trip had a profound impact on young Emily. She made new friends, many her age, who did not have a family. She carried their stories home with her, determined to do something to help. Upon her return home, Emily launched an intense and prolonged lobbying campaign bent on persuading her parents to consider adding to their family through adoption. While Mary Beth loved the idea of adoption, she didn't think it was for them. They already had three children and a very busy life. They had long considered themselves "done" following the birth of their youngest, Will. Steven sometimes joked when talking about his family onstage, "We have Eenie, Meenie, and Minie. And we hope to have no Mo."

Eventually, Emily won the day. The more the Chapmans prayed and considered this huge step, the more their hearts embraced the idea. The process took some time, but by January of 2000, the Chapmans found themselves signing the paperwork that put a beautiful treasure from China, Shaohannah Hope, into their loving arms.

So great was the joy and redemptive power they experienced in adding Shaohannah to their family, the Chapmans eventually adopted two more daughters from China. Stevey Joy's arrival in 2002 and Maria's in 2004 increased their clan to six children in all. But giving and loving came with a cost, and in 2008 the Chapman family also saw the loss of Maria in a tragic car accident when she was just five years old.

Not content to sit in their grief, the Chapmans wanted others to experience the joy of adoption. They recognized that the process of adoption was arduous and, of course, quite expensive. While they were grateful to be in a financial position that meant the high cost of adoption wasn't a barrier to following their hearts, they recognized that many others were not in such a position.

SEEING THE NEED OF OTHERS

Mary Beth became keenly aware that many other families desired to open up their hearts and families to a waiting child but were prohibited from doing so by the high cost. Everywhere she turned, she encountered friends, acquaintances, and strangers facing this daunting financial barrier.

Profoundly moved by this glaring need, Steven and Mary Beth cofounded a ministry they called Shaohannah's Hope (later renamed Show Hope). The organization was launched not only to increase awareness of the plight of children who had been orphaned but also to provide financial assistance to families with a longing to adopt. Never ambitious for the spotlight, leadership responsibility, or a complicated life, Mary Beth nevertheless found herself serving as president of the innovative nonprofit organization.

In her book *Choosing to SEE: A Story of Struggle and Hope*, Mary Beth explains, "There are about 140 million orphans in the world today. As we became aware of their needs, we read our Bibles with fresh eyes. We saw all the times that the Bible talks about both orphans and adoptions."[3]

Picking up on this theme, Mary Beth writes, "If there was ever an issue that followers of Jesus should be all about, it would be caring for orphans in their distress. So we've become increasingly involved in mobilizing churches and communities to care for orphans."[4]

Having navigated the complex adoption process three times herself and having been blessed with both a platform and resources, Mary Beth is uniquely equipped to lead other believers through the same maze and encourage them throughout their journey. Today Show Hope delivers this kind of help in four key areas.

The first involves meeting the need for which the ministry was founded—to help lower the high financial barrier for families who long to adopt. To that end, as we write, Show Hope has helped more than 5,800 children from more than sixty countries, including the United States, come home to loving families through Adoption Aid grants.

Show Hope also supports several Care Centers in China. Here they provide hope-filled care to orphans with acute medical and special needs. More than 2,500 children have received vital care through these centers.

Third, by leveraging Mary Beth's hard-won wisdom and experience with adoption, as well as that of scores of other couples, Show Hope provides support for parents both before and after bringing home their new, treasured family member through adoption.

Fourth, Show Hope's Student Initiatives empower students to engage in orphan care through various opportunities, including a global training curriculum and short-term trips to China. Through its programs, Show Hope has mobilized thousands of individuals, students, families, and churches to care for orphans by reducing barriers to adoption.

I (Jackie) realize that welcoming a child into one's family is a lifelong commitment of unconditional love, time, effort, and resources. Whether parenting a biological child or an adopted child, there is much giving required. My husband, Steve, and I believe it is a calling from God, not necessarily for every believer but supported in the Word.

Like the Chapmans, my husband and I thought we were done having children. In our book *This Dangerous Book: How the Bible Has Shaped Our World and Why It Still Matters Today* (Zondervan, 2017), I describe in more detail our family's adoption of a baby girl born in China. The seeds for adoption began with our own children, who believed God was calling us as a family to adopt. Through a divine set of circumstances and initially overcoming my apprehension, we came to adopt Gabi, who is now our delightful daughter and a special part of our family.

The journey started in 2004 at a hibachi dinner. We had five kids at the time, ranging from a senior in high school to a four-year-old. Steve and the kids had taken me out to dinner to celebrate my birthday. As we sat around the table, out of the blue one of our older girls said, "Mom, we think we need to adopt a baby from China!"

"Wow, I love adoption!" I replied. "But our lives are already so full." I explained to them that while I thought adoption was great, I did not feel a specific calling toward it. They wouldn't let it rest, though, so I told them I would think about it.

A few weeks later, at a Thanksgiving family get-together, one of the kids must have said something about that conversation to my mother, since she called me afterward, saying, "I hear you're planning on adopting." I assured her it was simply a discussion we'd had over dinner, then hung up the phone, called the kids into the room, and told them, "You can't tell people that we are going to adopt, because I don't know if it will ever happen."

"Please, Mom, will you at least pray about it?"

"All right, I'll pray about it, if you promise not to tell anyone else!"

That seemed to satisfy them, since they smiled at each other and left it at that.

Through the busy days of the holidays and my teens' basketball games, I didn't give the topic much thought or prayer. Then one January afternoon, my daughter Lindy came into the kitchen and asked if I had been praying about it. I confessed to her that I hadn't, but told her now that the holidays were over, I would start praying.

And I did. I read blogs on adoption, ordered books, and prayed. As I researched, adoption grew heavy on my heart. It would pop into my head as I went about my day, and I would start weeping. I called an agency and let them send me a packet. It started becoming real. The clincher came when I talked to Steve about it. We were out to dinner on one of our regular monthly date nights, and I asked him how he would feel about adopting. He put down his fork, looked at me, and said, "I could get really excited about it."

From that moment, I knew we would adopt.

A couple of months later, we went to an adoption workshop, where Steve filled out an application and signed the bottom line. I knew we were supposed to adopt, but I still had hesitations. That was on a Saturday night.

The next morning, I woke up early to get everyone ready for church, and I fervently asked God to give me clarity. A man from our church who had no idea we were contemplating adoption stopped Steve after the worship service.

"I was raised in a Baptist church," our friend said, "and I don't know much about the whole 'word from the Lord' kind of thing. But last week in my Bible study, I felt like God told me, 'There's a blessing for Steve and Jackie in China,' so whatever you're doing, keep doing it."

When I heard his message, I was amazed. No question about it, God wanted us to adopt. Less than two years later, we were picking up our little girl to bring her home! The day we met her, she was ten and a half months old. The orphanage director brought her to the door and called our names, and our sweet baby girl smiled and reached out to us like she had been waiting for us to get there. We named her Gabriella, which means "Woman of God" and "God is my strength." Now, eleven years later, we can't imagine our lives without her!

As an adoptive family, we understand the faith journey that adoption can be. It can be long, frustrating, financially straining, and anxiety ridden. When we were in the midst of the two-year process, I felt like that was the biggest faith journey I had ever been on. God had time to teach us a lot of valuable lessons during the long wait. I learned to trust God for my baby's care and protection while she was half a world away. We prayed for our daughter that we chose to love without even seeing her or knowing her. She didn't have to earn our love. Isn't that how God loves us? Through adopting, we now have a better understanding of how God adopted us into His family.

CONTAGIOUS GENEROSITY

So what's the point? What do we learn? No doubt, adoption is a wonderful form of generosity, but the impact of that kind of giving spreads beyond the adoptive family. When we experience generosity in our lives, there's something captivating and contagious about it. We want to share it with others.

That's the way God's love works. And oh, how we need to let His love penetrate our hearts! Mary Beth Chapman saw the power of three little girls whose lives were changed. Her eyes were opened to their needs, igniting a deep passion in Mary Beth's heart to make it possible for more kids to enter families, just as her children had.

Her giving continues to produce an ever-growing legacy: thousands of children growing up in Christian homes across America.

That is the nature of legacies. Their fullest manifestations come long after we have gone. Theologian Elton Trueblood had this truth in mind when he wrote, "A man has made at least a start on discovering the meaning of human life when he plants shade trees under which he knows full well he will never sit."[5]

A generous life is a life well lived. And living out generosity starts by viewing everything we have through the lens of stewardship. Our possessions, our finances, even our lives are not our own. Rather they belong to God. We have been given the opportunity to steward our time, talents, and resources. When we consider everything to be God's and see the responsibility to steward it wisely, we can begin to live out generosity with greater depth and meaning. We will not take anything with us when we leave this world, so why not generously invest in those things that will live on past us—men's and women's souls and God's Word. Lasting impact is driven by what we are willing to give away. Generosity marks the woman of legacy, fueled by gratitude and a profound sense of eternity.

CHAPTER 3

THE LEGACY OF WITNESS

One faithful witness is worth a thousand mute professors of religion . . . Our faith grows by expression . . . we must share it—we must witness.

—Billy Graham[1]

Jesus told people who'd experienced healing or salvation to go home and testify to their family, their friends, their community. He knew that there's nothing more powerful than the account from a firsthand participant. And in the most critical moment of human history—the resurrection—God used a woman as the first witness to the event.

The Woman as Witness

Picture the moment. Mary Magdalene is inconsolable. Through her sobs, she attempts to explain to a huddle of Jesus' disciples what she and some of the Master's other female followers have just witnessed.

Arising before dawn, they made their way through Jerusalem's empty streets toward the garden tomb, carrying anointing oils, spices, and other supplies necessary for a proper Jewish burial. Arriving at the burial place, they found the massive stone barrier moved away from the opening, and the tomb itself empty. Assuming that the body had been stolen by the same cruel tormenters who had arranged to have Jesus crucified, Mary left the other women behind and ran as fast as she could back to the house where the terrified and confused disciples were hiding.

After hearing her breathless report of what happened, two of those disciples, Peter and John, bolt for the door and head to see for themselves. Here on this Sunday morning, the two men will find the scene just as Mary Magdalene described it.

After recovering both her breath and her composure, Mary decides to rejoin the others at the tomb. If there is to be a search for the body, she wants to be part of it. Going back to the same place, she finds it empty! Neither the other women nor the two men are anywhere to be seen. Alone and confused, she is overwhelmed by the sight of the rolled-away stone and memories of Friday's horrifying events, and she starts to sob once more.

Through her tears, she thinks she sees something. *Is that a glimmer of light coming from inside the sepulcher?* She calls in through the low doorway of the tomb. She hears only silence in response. Cautiously, she stoops and leans to peer in through the opening. What she sees causes her to gasp.

Two of the tallest men she has ever seen, dressed in brilliant white, sit at either end of the rock-hewn shelf that had cradled Jesus' broken, linen-wrapped body. She stares for a few seconds, frozen in astonishment, and then startles again when one of the men speaks.

"Dear woman, why are you crying?"

She manages to stammer out a response. "Because they have taken away my Lord, and I do not know where they have put Him."

She must find the others, so she exits the tomb. Blinking and squinting in the bright morning light, she sees the figure of a third man, also dressed in white, standing in the garden courtyard. She approaches the man but, in accordance with Jewish customs of the day, keeps her eyes lowered to avoid eye contact with a strange man. As she approaches, the man asks her two questions.

"Dear woman, why are you crying? Who are you looking for?"

Still avoiding the man's face, Mary feels a surge of desperate boldness. "Sir, if you have taken Him away, tell me where you have put Him, and I will go and get Him."

The stranger replies with a single word that electrifies her soul and will transform the rest of her life.

"Mary!"

That voice. No one spoke her name like He did. No other lips could communicate compassion and power the way His did. There is no mistaking it. Somehow . . . some way . . . the man she helped prepare for burial on Friday evening is standing here before her on Sunday morning.

She runs to Him and throws her arms around Him, but He gently pulls away. "Don't cling to me," He says, "for I haven't yet ascended to the Father. But go find my brothers and tell them, 'I am ascending to my Father and your Father, to my God and your God.'"

Mary had trudged to this garden tomb under a crushing weight of grief and disappointment. Now she runs with unspeakable joy to bring others some wonderful news. She has seen Him. She has spoken with Him. This woman with a past has been granted the extraordinary honor of being the first person on earth to bear witness to the most significant event in human history.

"He lives."

THE UNIQUE WITNESS OF WOMEN

It cannot be coincidental that the first people to learn that Christ had conquered death were women. Mary was the first to see

Him. But the women who traveled to the tomb with Mary that morning and lingered behind as Mary rushed back heard an angelic announcement of the resurrection as well: "The women were terrified and bowed with their faces to the ground. Then the men asked, 'Why are you looking among the dead for someone who is alive? He isn't here! He is risen from the dead! Remember what he told you back in Galilee, that the Son of Man must be betrayed into the hands of sinful men and be crucified, and that he would rise again on the third day.' Then they remembered that he had said this. So they rushed back from the tomb to tell his eleven disciples—and everyone else—what had happened" (Luke 24:5–9 NLT).

Why does God use these women as the first witnesses of the risen Lord? The difference between the men and women in the story is revealing. The women stand at the tomb weeping. They *feel* the loss. And even when the women come and tell the disciples that Jesus is risen, the Scriptures tell us the men do not believe, "because their words seemed to them like nonsense" (Luke 24:11). The men respond logically and have to go check it out for themselves.

Consider what would have happened if God had not wired the women to respond with emotion and compassion. Perhaps their words would have been dismissed or overlooked. The disciples might well have stayed home. That resurrection morning, it was the women who first saw what was happening and fully grasped and appreciated it. God uniquely wires and calls women as witnesses. Our ability to respond in the moment makes us uniquely equipped to share with others the stories of God's grace, mercy, and hope in our lives.

THE CALL TO WITNESS
The unique wiring of empathy, compassion, and responding in the moment allows us to fulfill our call as female witnesses of

God in our lives. The great thing about God and His calling is that He never requires any special certifications, just availability. We testify—we witness—to what we've seen and heard. We don't need to have a special message, speech, or declaration. Mary's testimony was so simple: "He lives."

Our challenge is to accept the calling and then to respond with boldness. To be a witness requires courage. It often means standing against the tide of popular opinion and the latest cultural fashions or trends. As the amazing pioneering missionary to India Amy Carmichael (1867–1951) reminds us, "If I am afraid to speak the truth lest I lose affection, or lest the one concerned should say, 'You do not understand,' or because I fear to lose my reputation for kindness; if I put my own good name before the other's highest good, then I know nothing of Calvary's love."[2]

It might require some bravery, but what a lasting legacy through witness does not require is eloquent speaking skills or an encyclopedic knowledge of God's Word. Your story of God's grace is *your* story. And no one else can tell it.

Can anyone be a witness? Consider the story of an unassuming woman who followed her heart for the lost and broken of this world and found herself the mother of a global phenomenon.

The Witness of Action

He was a drunk. As he staggered down the road, a gang of older boys taunted and harassed him while a policeman stood idly by. Nine-year-old Catherine Mumford, while shy and quiet, could not stand the scene. She rushed to the man's side, scolded the boys, and took the man's arm to offer support. The little girl accompanied him and the policeman all the way to the police station, even as neighbors stared in shock and disapproval.

This story was just the beginning of her witness.

In Catherine's teen years, she suffered from curvature of

the spine that kept her confined to her home. Instead of self-pity, she turned to voracious reading of evangelical leaders of the day, including Charles Finney and James Caughey from the United States and the Wesleys from England. This study provided grounding for her later witness.

Years later, in 1852, while attending Bible study in the home of a friend, Catherine Mumford met the man she would one day marry. William Booth had traveled to her hometown to preach at her church. Even at their first meeting, they both knew they were meant for each other. After Booth departed her hometown, they continued a regular stream of correspondence until they were married three years later.

Not only had the twenty-three-year-old woman been powerfully drawn to an evangelist, but in her chest beat the heart of an evangelist as well. Both loved God and possessed a remarkable love for hurting people who did not know Him. The term "sinners"—as they were called in that day—has fallen out of favor today, though when Catherine and William Booth spoke of their concern for sinners, the word carried the fragrance of compassion and concern. Catherine Booth knew that sin ravages the person God loves—both body and soul. It seemed she had always known this.

Catherine's burden to see people who were trapped in sin find freedom only increased as she matured. She also believed that women could and should lead in this quest to save those who were hopeless, helpless, and lost. In one of her many letters to William during their long engagement, she made known her desire to stand right beside men in the fight for people's souls. Reflecting this passion, she would one day write, "Cast off all bonds of prejudice and custom, and let the love of Christ, which is in you, have free course to run out in all conceivable schemes and methods of labour for the souls of men."[3]

In the early years of their ministry, Catherine stayed largely in the background, quietly supporting her husband's ministry activities. They moved to a lower-class section of London, where she periodically taught a children's Bible class or spoke at a women's group, but a general shyness and reticence about being in a public position characterized her approach to ministry.

That all changed one night as she walked along a city street to meet her husband for an evening church service. As she walked, she could see into the windows of several of the dilapidated row houses where small groups of people seemed to be chatting, gossiping, and passing the time. As she took in the scene, she sensed the Spirit of God moving within her. A wave of compassion broke over her, along with a powerful urge to introduce them to the God she loved. A voice within her spoke: *Would you not be doing God more service, and acting more like your Redeemer, by turning into some of these houses, speaking to these careless sinners, and inviting them to the service, than by going to enjoy it yourself?*

She knew the answer. Standing on that London sidewalk, Catherine looked to heaven and breathed a prayer for boldness. Then she approached a group of women sitting on the stoop of a nearby row house. The women did not embrace her invitation, but neither did they reject or belittle Catherine. With newfound confidence, she walked up to the next door and shared the love of Christ with the people there.

In that moment, the seeds of a new kind of evangelistic ministry were planted. They grew into a strategy for outreach that brought preaching *to* lost and hurting people rather than expecting those people to find their way to a church. William and Catherine Booth were already regularly on the streets ministering to derelict alcoholics. Yes, the nine-year-old girl who rushed to steady and protect a stumbling drunk had not lost her compassionate instincts in womanhood. Soon the couple started going into the slums of London's East End twice each week to preach the gospel to people who had never heard it. Describing this strategy, Catherine wrote, "More than two-thirds of the working classes never cross the threshold of a church or chapel. It is evident that if they are to be reached, extraordinary means must be employed."[4]

True to their goals and vision, the bulk of William and Catherine's ministry in those early days was to alcoholics, morphine addicts, prostitutes, and other social outcasts.

Catherine's "extraordinary means" eventually became the East End Christian Mission. As the work rapidly expanded to other areas and cities, the name was shortened to simply the Christian Mission, and then ultimately, in 1878, was changed to the Salvation Army. William then took the title of general, rather than pastor or director. Catherine became widely known as the Mother of the Salvation Army.

Witnessing takes many forms, however. Catherine also became the principal fundraiser for their organization. The formerly meek and timid woman stood before Britain's wealthiest Christians, raising funds for the dual mission of delivering practical help and gospel hope to the poor and broken. At the time of the name change, the Salvation Army employed 127 full-time ministers, many of whom had been saved and transformed through the mission's outreaches, and had a network of affiliated churches and meeting houses with attendance of more than 27,000 on a typical Sunday night. Catherine accomplished all this while raising eight children, all of whom entered full-time ministry. The work expanded further from there, vaulting the Atlantic and Pacific to take root in North America and in Australia as well, eventually operating in 127 countries and communicating in 175 languages.

For more than 150 years, the Salvation Army has stood as a witness to God's love and saving grace to the world's most destitute individuals. Catherine started at nine years of age with a man in need, then obediently took one step forward at each opportunity along the way.

We know Catherine was legacy minded. When asked about the often-unorthodox methods the Salvation Army employed in reaching the unreached, she would frequently respond, "There is no improving the future without disturbing the present."[5] Is there a future you'd like to have? If so, perhaps there's a present reality that needs disturbing.

We'd like to introduce you to a contemporary woman we're confident Catherine Booth would have seen as a kindred spirit.

The Unlikely Legacy

Legacy often starts in unlikely places. Neither of us would have anticipated sharing our own story on a public stage. If anyone had told either one of us that we'd stand to speak to hundreds, even thousands, we'd have said they were crazy. We are assuming that is true for you too and that perhaps you can identify with the unlikely legacy of Marilyn Hickey.

Marilyn's journey found its beginnings in the Great Depression in the northwest corner of the Texas panhandle. Her childhood years in Dalhart, Texas, placed her in the center of the notorious Dust Bowl at its height. She came to Christ as a teenager and in her twenties met and married a young pastor, Wally Hickey.

She seemed destined to play the vital but often low-profile role of a pastor's wife. But then she began leading women's Bible studies, and a powerful teaching gift became evident. Her studies grew in popularity and led to regular speaking opportunities. She started a radio ministry that grew to be national, and then global, in scope. This in a time that hadn't heard a nationally prominent woman Bible teacher on radio since Aimee Semple McPherson in the 1920s. Television eventually joined radio as a key element in Marilyn's pioneering outreach. She found herself an integral part of several of the key spiritual developments of the '60s and '70s, including the Jesus movement, the Full Gospel Business Men's Fellowship phenomenon, and the charismatic renewal movement. This resulted in an ongoing global platform for nurturing emerging Christian leaders.

In the early 1980s, Marilyn connected with a young evangelical church in Budapest, Hungary, and began teaching there on a regular basis, even while that nation was still behind the Iron Curtain. Today Budapest's Faith Church ministers to more than sixty thousand people each weekend in its satellite locations across Hungary. You'll find thriving churches all over the planet—from Egypt to Ethiopia to China to Brazil—that view Hickey as a mentor and spiritual mother.

After Marilyn and her husband, Wally, had labored and pastored together for fifty-eight years, he passed away. Nevertheless, well into her eighties, Marilyn Hickey continues to travel the world teaching, preaching, and training church leaders.

On just a single night in December of 2016, at the age of eighty-five, Marilyn preached the gospel to a throng of roughly one million Pakistanis in Karachi, Pakistan. That evening, as Marilyn invited her audience to receive Christ as Savior, hundreds of thousands stood to pray with her. This stands as only one milestone event in a remarkable, decades-long journey of bearing testimony to the saving, redeeming power of Christ. During that same trip, she also held a two-day training workshop for more than five thousand Pakistani pastors and lay leaders.

Ministry in predominantly Islamic nations has been a major point of focus for her in recent years. In an era in which many Christians have written off Muslim nations as hopeless cases for the gospel, Marilyn has been seeking and finding open doors there. She has met with high-ranking imams in both Pakistan and Egypt, engaging in respectful dialogue about the Jesus of the

Bible. Her 2012 book *Dinner with Muhammad: A Surprising Look at a Beautiful Friendship* reveals Marilyn's heart and strategy for Muslim evangelism. On two occasions, she has offered to pray for ailing spouses of prominent Muslim clerics and seen God touch them in remarkable ways. In her book, she writes, "Muslims are very open to prayer, and even though they usually know nothing about the Bible, they revere it as a holy book. Anytime I get the chance to say to a Muslim, 'May I pray for you in the name of Jesus?' I consider it a wonderful opportunity. They love prayer and they certainly love prayer in the name of Jesus."[6]

All of these things stand as evidence of what is already a remarkable legacy as a witness for Christ, and Marilyn shows no signs of slowing down. She has mentored or inspired some of the most impactful individuals in ministry today.

It might be easy to look at the worldwide travel, the radio and TV ministry, and forget Marilyn's origins, but it should not be forgotten where she began: as a Depression-era Dust Bowl woman. Her aspirations were not to be spotlighted on the stage. She was committed to being a pastor's wife.

She had a hunger for God's Word, and she had a hunger to study. Both of those traits gave her a desire to teach, and as she taught, she saw God produce the results. This description of a woman with a hunger for God's Word and a hunger for study can be used to describe many women. That's where we must all remain faithful—in our sphere of influence and in our willingness to act when prompted to bear witness to His great name.

WITNESS IN EVERY SEASON

A long time ago, the Bible tells us, John the Baptist was raised up as the forerunner to Jesus. He went to the wilderness and preached repentance and baptized many. The crowds came out, and it must have been quite the sight to see this evangelist dressed in camel's hair, eating locusts and honey. Eventually, though, as

Jesus came onto the scene, the crowds began to drift away from John. They went to see Jesus, who was performing great miracles.

How easy it would have been for John the Baptist to sulk, to even seek to hold on to his position. His disciples questioned this turn of events: "Rabbi, that man who was with you on the other side of the Jordan—the one you testified about—look, he is baptizing, and everyone is going to him" (John 3:26).

John's response was wise beyond human understanding. He told them, "A person can receive only what is given them from heaven" (John 3:27). In humility, John recognized that he had no reason to be jealous or hold on to his fame, since his ministry had always been a gift from God. John's answer is a powerful legacy-building statement. Each of us has been given one life from God, and we have the opportunity to respond to this gift the same way John did. If we are faithful with what God gives us, He will give us a lasting legacy, whether it is as a speaker, a housewife, a teacher, or a factory worker.

Witnessing is lived out differently in each season of life. God gives different roles for different seasons, and each position is not for us to hold on to but rather for us to use to show the world God's goodness.

My friend Casey Yates and I (Lauren) are examples of witness in different seasons of life. Casey and I met when we were seven years old. Only being a day apart in age, we decided when we were ten years old that we should celebrate our birthdays with joint parties. Now, twenty years later, we still celebrate with joint parties every year! We have so many memories growing up together through grade school, middle school, and high school. Once we finished up high school, Casey and I both attended the University of Oklahoma and even joined the same sorority. I guess you could say we have loved doing life together!

After college, Casey got a master's degree in speech pathology and then worked full-time as a speech pathologist, helping children and infants with hearing loss. I loved seeing her care for the children she worked with and encouraging their families. She worked in this role for a number of years, until she had her first child. Once her daughter was born, Casey began her own practice for in-home speech therapy, which allowed her to work part-time and be home with her daughter more.

As seasons of life change, I have watched Casey consistently live with great intentionality and purpose, first as a full-time speech pathologist and now as a wife and mother. Whatever her context, she is living in light of a long-term legacy. I've seen her gracefully wrestle through the transition between seasons, with a desire to make the most of what God has given her.

Casey loves on her husband and daughter so well, and she also loves on everyone else she comes into contact with. She sacrifices her time and comfort in order to serve her community by getting involved in one of our church's outreach programs: providing school supplies to the local elementary school students and delivering snacks to the teachers. She goes out for coffee or lunch with other new moms to encourage them, writes encouraging posts for the women's ministry blog, and uses her time to show God's love wherever she is. Casey is creating a legacy through living intentionally even as her life changes.

While Casey is faithfully living out her role as a full-time mama and part-time speech pathologist, God has given me a different witness for this season, one equally important. My husband, Michael, and I have been wrestling for three years with infertility. We've also been pursuing adoption for nearly six years now, unsuccessfully. Casey and I had planned and hoped to start our families at the same time. Now, years later, she has just had her second child, while I haven't been able to have children as I had hoped.

Through this difficult season, one I never planned for, I get to choose what kind of witness I want to be. Michael and I have decided to be open with others about our experience with infertility, in the hope of providing encouragement to people who may find themselves in a similar situation. As I've been open about our experience, I am incredibly humbled when others are willing to trust us with their own stories. When I connect with others on this level, I get to share my faith journey with them and tell them how God's Word has been my strength in this season. It has been a joy to relate to others, pray with them, and encourage them to look to Christ for their comfort and hope. Through it all, I can honestly say that God is still good, even though our lives look different than what we expected. There is deep comfort and peace knowing that God is with us and has a plan for our lives.

This unique season of life is not one I ever would have asked for, but I can see how God is using it as a testimony to his love.

Of course, Michael and I still have the grief. The pain of childlessness is a particular pain, described by one couple as "the grief which has no focus for its tears and no object for its love."[7] I still have days that are more difficult than others. But in those days, as Michael and I go to God, to each other, and to our community for strength and comfort, we continue to trust God and pray that in the process, we will build our witness more than ever. We can say with confidence that with or without children, we have Jesus, and He is enough.

Witness is seen when we live out our faith and speak of God's truth, wherever He has placed us in life. As with Mary Magdalene at the outset of this chapter, our witness cannot be underestimated. Mary's simple proclamation of faith, "He lives," sent the disciples running. And perhaps, as with Mary, our simple proclamations of faith—wherever we are, wherever God has put us—will rock the world around us.

CHAPTER 4

THE LEGACY OF WISDOM

A pattern of wise choices in the ordinary
paves the road to a demonstration of wisdom
in the extraordinary.

—Lysa TerKeurst[1]

How does a woman rise to power, influence, and even military command in a male-dominated society? The answer is simply wisdom.

Consider it. The entire nation of Israel has turned from God. They have nothing to unify them; the period of the kings is still two hundred years away. The scribes' record of this period in Israel's history is that every person simply did "whatever seemed right in their own eyes" (Judg. 21:25 NLT).

This disobedience and lack of unity has left them vulnerable to attack and oppression by neighboring Canaanite warlords. One cruel despot in particular—Jabin of Hazor, aided by his military commander, Sisera—has terrorized God's people for two decades, making their lives a misery of deprivation and fear. The Bible records that in their despair the people of Israel cried out for help.

The Rise of Deborah

In this hopeless and desperate situation, God raises up not a man but a woman named Deborah. She's described as a prophetess as well as the wife of Lappidoth (Judg. 4:4). Both of those things tell you something.

A prophet was God's spokesperson to the people. Deborah was so identified as a prophet that she stood out enough to be recognized, even by the men of her nation, as capable of leading. While the Bible is silent as to Deborah's story before she became a prophetess, we can rest assured that her position did not come as the result of casual study. Here was a woman devoted to God and His Word.

She was also the wife of Lappidoth. Now, the Bible doesn't really tell us anything about Lappidoth. It would have been easy enough not to include this fact, yet the Scriptures are intentional in recording this. Deborah's rise to prominence was not at the cost of her marriage; she didn't forget her ties to her husband. Instead both were wonderfully woven together—a celebration of her wisdom and her marriage.

DEBORAH'S WISDOM IN ACTION

Deborah is the first and only female judge in the history of Israel. The people regularly come to her "under the Palm of Deborah between Ramah and Bethel in the hill country of Ephraim" (Judg. 4:5). On most days, people from all across the territories of the twelve tribes of Israel journey to this spot seeking counsel or dispute resolution. However, it is not enough to provide wisdom to the people. There is war and oppression; Jabin of Hazor and Sisera, the commander of his army, with the power of their nine hundred chariots, are bent on Israel's destruction.

How will she step into the battle?

If Deborah is to serve as Israel's new Moses, leading her people out of bondage, she will need to find her Joshua, a military field commander to lead a makeshift army cobbled together from among the farmers and craftsmen of the tribes. Deborah is aware of the impossibility of this mission—a small force against

nine hundred chariots. Nonetheless, she finds a willing prospect in Barak of the tribe of Naphtali. And here it's noteworthy
that Deborah wisely charges and inspires Barak with God's
word: "Has not the LORD, the God of Israel, commanded you,
'Go, gather your men at Mount Tabor, taking 10,000 from the
people of Naphtali and the people of Zebulun. And I will draw
out Sisera, the general of Jabin's army, to meet you by the river
Kishon with his chariots and his troops, and I will give him into
your hand'?" (Judg. 4:6–7 ESV).

Backed by the encouragement that victory is assured, Barak
raises an army of ten thousand men. The first act of this new
force is to defeat and expel the raping, robbing Canaanite raid-
ing parties plaguing the area. Word of this Israelite uprising
quickly reaches Jabin, and he immediately dispatches the full
force of his military might to crush it. Israelite scouts report that
the dreaded nine hundred iron chariots and a sea of foot soldiers
are headed toward Ephraim.

Deborah's hill is largely deserted on that day. No long line of
litigants await her judgment or counsel. Only her military commander, Barak, stands with her. He is fully prepared to take his
men into battle against the Canaanites, but he has one demand.
Deborah must accompany them. His men want to know she is
with them. He needs her too. The certainty of her prophecy fills
them all with confidence and courage. Deborah assents. She will
join them on the battlefield.

Before the sun sets, the people of Israel will have won a great
victory. The enemy will be so shattered that peace and prosper-
ity will characterize the lives of an entire generation of Israelites
in this region. Afterward Deborah and Barak will cowrite a victory anthem that will be recorded in the fifth chapter of Judges
and still be read by twenty-first-century Bible readers more than
three thousand years later. Among the stanzas of this exultant
hymn we find:

> There were few people left in the villages of Israel—
> until Deborah arose as a mother for Israel. . . .
> Then there was peace in the land for forty years.
>
> —Judges 5:7, 31 NLT

THE LEGACY OF DEBORAH'S WISDOM

"Until Deborah arose as a mother for Israel."

As a female military leader, Deborah holds a unique place in the biblical narrative and indeed in all of ancient history. Only the warrior-queen Boudicca, who battled the invading Romans in first-century Britain, rivals her exploits. The difference is that brave Boudicca died in battle for a failing cause. Deborah, on the other hand, used godly wisdom to lead her people into a season of security, and she left us a legacy that still survives. At a time in Israel's history when the people were fragmented, disorganized, visionless, and suffering, Deborah stepped up to provide the one thing they needed most: wise leadership.

Like all wise leaders, she knew she couldn't do everything herself. It was critical that she recruit the right people to her cause. She convinced Barak that he was the right man to command the ragtag army, helping him believe in himself and bolstering his faith in a God who gives victory to underdogs.

There are 1,189 chapters in the Bible, and only two are devoted to Deborah's actions. Even so, more than three thousand years later they remain a rich source of wisdom and insight for women willing to be used by God to restore and defend their communities.

Deborah arose at a dark time in Israel's history. The nation had turned its back on God. His chosen people were polarized, passive, and fearful. A fog of compromise and despair had settled over the land. Generations earlier, their forefathers had entered this land of promise with such lofty, God-planted dreams of building a nation where they, the liberated slaves of Egypt, could be free and prosperous. Over several centuries, the memory of that dream faded. Crime devastated the economy as lawlessness turned once-happy villages into ghost towns.

> There were few people left in the villages of Israel—until Deborah arose as a mother for Israel . . .

We too live in a culture that has seemingly lost its way. Good people in many of our communities and neighborhoods feel they're under siege. Many are stressed out and even fearful. Many sense a spirit of lawlessness on the rise.

In every era, dark times place a demand on good women to rise up and lead others in righting societal wrongs and curing cultural ills. The bottom line is, in every generation we need women like Deborah who are willing to dig deep into God's Word and proclaim it.

When a culture finds itself desolate and oppressed, perhaps it's time for the "mothers" to arise. Isn't this what we're seeing right now among the Kurdish and Yazidi women of northern Iraq? After thousands of their mothers, sisters, and daughters have been kidnapped and raped by ISIS, the remaining women are banding together and training as combat soldiers to go out in defense of their people. They would rather die fighting alongside their husbands and sons than be forced into sexual slavery at the hands of ISIS.

Of course, the plight of the Kurds and Yazidis of Iraq and Syria is an extreme case, one deserving of our prayers and attention. The perils they face are grave beyond imagination.

Yet in a similar way, our times are calling for all Christian women to rouse themselves and hear a call to defend what is under attack and restore what has been desolated.

Often when I (Jackie) confront a situation in which I know

wisdom is required, I find myself feeling anxious. Does that ever happen to you? Over the years, I've learned to use that uneasy feeling as a cue to press into God and His Word.

The Bible is wisdom at our fingertips. I've seen it over and over in my life. True wisdom can be defined as knowing and applying the Word of God. Our culture has declined to such a degree that we have abandoned the biblical wisdom that many previous generations took for granted. People today think they have the answers, but they don't. I am grateful that I have something bigger than myself and my own ideas to look to. Having the Bible readily available is a tremendous gift.

For millennia, God's people have leaned on the ancient Scriptures and found wisdom for their situations. The Bible is as relevant today as it was when it was recorded by those chosen and inspired by God to deliver His infallible, inerrant, living Word to mankind. We will be wise women in our own day to the degree that we are women of the Word.

While we won't be taking up arms like Deborah, we can and must take to our knees. The prayer of a godly woman "avails much" (James 5:16 NKJV), but we wield even greater power when we pray together, united with faith and purpose.

Finding the Hidden Wisdom

Some women are recognized for their wisdom in their own lifetimes, as we've celebrated in Deborah's story. Their wisdom propels them to positions of leadership or earns them wide influence.

There are others who display their wisdom in the everyday context of work, school, family, or church. They speak, grounded in God's Word, and people recognize their wisdom, even if it doesn't generate any newspaper headlines. But that's the beauty of wisdom. It still holds its value whether one person or one million people receive it. We'd like you to consider one such woman—Sarah Haggar Osborn—whose wisdom was not recognized until years later.

It's likely you have never heard of her. When you read her story, she sounds like many women of today who've had to wrestle with poor marriages, little income, and single parenting. Yet if you are an evangelical Christian, you are a beneficiary and product of her influence, particularly if you are an American evangelical.

THE BEGINNING OF THE ORDINARY

Sarah was born to devout Puritan parents in England in 1714. The family moved to the colonies in America when she was a small child, and they settled in Rhode Island. She married at seventeen and very soon was widowed when her husband died suddenly in their second year of marriage, leaving her penniless with an infant son.

She remarried quickly, partly out of desperation, but this husband proved to be unstable and unreliable. After some sort of mental or emotional breakdown, he never worked again. Sarah was left to find a way to support herself and her children. Her diaries from this season describe her struggles to obtain food and firewood in order to sustain her young children.

As if these challenges weren't enough, she suffered from the early onset of some sort of painful, ongoing health condition that could not be identified. Modern doctors have studied her descriptions of her symptoms and narrowed down her likely condition to either rheumatoid arthritis or multiple sclerosis. Whatever it was, it made battling through pain a part of her daily existence.

To survive, she opened a small boarding school in Newport, in which she worked as the sole teacher as well as administrator, custodian, laundress, and cook for ten boarders plus several dozen day students.

Let's pause for a moment. In the face of seemingly impossible circumstances, rather than surrender to despair, she became an entrepreneur. Where some saw challenges, she saw an opportunity, and she summoned all of her resources and creativity to make the most of it. She took over a neighbor's boarding school and began to promote it throughout the region. Think about that. She was marketing a start-up enterprise—in 1758! This despite criticism from within her community. A working mother was unheard of in colonial-era America. Disapproving neighbors assumed that her efforts to earn money would take her away from her family responsibilities. Yet what other choice did she have?

Sarah displayed the grit of the working woman long before it was common for women to work outside the home. In Sarah's later years, as many as five hundred people would pass through her home during the course of a week to hear her teach and respond to questions about the life of faith. Even though she was uncredentialed, many traveled great distances to sit and hear her thoughts. However, her biggest audience was still to come.

THE BEGINNINGS OF THE WISDOM LEGACY

In the face of all her hardships, Sarah maintained a fierce devotion to God, and in every spare waking moment she poured out her thoughts, prayers, and convictions onto paper. She hoped one day her writings would have an impact, but she had no guarantee. In marked humility and wisdom, she wrote, "If a word in these lines ever prove useful to one soul after my decease it will be ten thousand times more than I deserve from the hands of a bountiful God, to him alone be all the glory."[2]

We might not ever have had a deep look into this amazing woman's heart except for the fact that, fortunately, Sarah was an epic journaler long before journaling was a thing. And we mean *epic*. At the age of twenty-nine, she wrote a complete memoir of her life and spiritual journey. In spite of raising children, operating a boarding school, and experiencing daily health issues, Sarah somehow found the time to fill fifty volumes of writing—more than fifteen thousand pages! She poured her thoughts onto sheets of parchment with quill and ink and then hand-bound them by stitching them with her pain-racked fingers. More than two centuries later, her stitches on the surviving journals remain tight and neat.

Sadly, for various reasons including a house fire, only two thousand pages of her writings survived, but those that remain are filled with remarkable biblical wisdom and insight. She wrote powerfully and persuasively on themes that were also the hallmarks of an emergent evangelical faith in this era, and her passion for the gospel was evident: "I sincerely aim and the good of my own soul as a means to stir up gratitude in the most ungrateful of all hearts, even mine, to a glorious and compassionate Saviour for all his benefit toward so vile a monster in sin as I am and for the encouragement of any who may providentially light on these lines after my decease to trust in the Lord and never despair of his mercy."[3]

Her written pages began circulating to a broader audience around the same time that the preaching of men like John Wesley, George Whitefield, Gilbert Tennent, and others was sparking revival fires throughout the colonies. In these texts, she was passionate about the miracle of conversion and the opportunity for any individual to enjoy a personal relationship with a good and loving Father. She wrote about the power and necessity of God's grace, in contrast to religious striving and human effort. She was compelled to commit to paper the faith she held so tightly.

Sarah Osborn died in 1796, twenty years and one month after the signing of the Declaration of Independence. She was eighty-two, frail, and nearly blind. She left behind almost nothing of material value. After her death, it was her journals—her writings—that became most prized.

Her substantial legacy is built exclusively on the thousands of neatly sewn journal pages and, of course, on the lives and legacies of the people she encouraged with her wisdom. She wrote for Christ, and her writing's impact has stretched long beyond her own life and into eternity.

On the cover of one of those diaries, she inked a dedication of sorts. She placed the words she had written at "the disposal of Providence." Her prayer of consecration was essentially, "Lord, do with these writings as you see fit." Biographer Catherine Brekus studied Sarah's many letters and came away convinced of this: "Her most cherished hope was that someday her manuscripts would be read by people who shared her hunger to communicate with a personal, majestic, sovereign God."[4]

They were, and they made Sarah Osborn a woman of legacy through hard-won wisdom.

Like Sarah Osborn, I (Lauren) have found great value in journaling. As I write this, I am reflecting on the excitement I felt last night as I filled the last page of yet another journal. That means I got to pick out a fresh, new blank journal that will be with me over the next few months as I fill its pages. I made the commitment to journaling daily back in November 2004, and I haven't stopped since. Every night as a part of my routine, I sit in bed with a pen and journal in hand and write. I always do this after I've finished my daily Bible reading. I reflect on the day's reading, and I also write out my prayers as a way to work through my life seasons, whether good or bad. Over the years of journaling my prayers, I've come to have a unique ritual of writing my prayers in cursive, while I print anything else. It's a small distinction that, for me, signals a shift in my posture of the heart. For me, journaling is a therapeutic process, and it helps me pursue Jesus to greater depths.

Sarah Osborn's example reminds us of a Sarah in our day who turned a habit of journaling in her quiet times with God into writings that have impacted millions around the world. Her journal entries took the form of a devotional that became a runaway global bestseller.

Sarah Young and her husband spent many years on the mission field in Japan and Australia. Throughout that time, Sarah practiced a form of interaction with God not unlike that of Sarah Osborn. She would pour out her feelings, thoughts, and questions to Jesus in her prayer journals. Then one year she was inspired to upend that process. In her prayer times, she began to sit quietly before the Lord and invite the Spirit of God to communicate to her spirit what Jesus would say to her. She would faithfully write down what she sensed God was saying to her.

In 2004, excerpts from those journals were published in the form of a 365-day devotional titled *Jesus Calling*. The project became an international publishing phenomenon. By 2017, the book had sold more than seventeen million copies worldwide in various formats.

Sarah Young is quick to point out that no devotional and no journaling exercise can take the place of the Bible as the highest authority for the believer and ultimate arbiter of spiritual truth. She has said that her devotional books "are meant to be read slowly, preferably in a quiet place, with your Bible open."[5]

As we see in the lives of both Sarah Osborn and Sarah Young, there is tremendous power in just being faithful before God. We've all been dealt different circumstances in our lives. The question is, What will we choose to do with them? This is where we need wisdom. Just as Deborah knew, and Sarah Osborn, and Sarah Young after her, no greater wisdom can be found than in the Word of God. Wise women look to Scripture as the source of all truth for living, able to guide all our ways.

Some of us may fill endless journals that never see the light of day, but the fruit of those efforts should not be overlooked. The discipline of inward reflection, listening to God, and writing in response produces insight that impacts others. Truly, the gentle encouragement to go deep with our Lord cultivates the soil that will bring a harvest to people around us.

Sometimes, however, our stories, even if we are members of royalty, take a far different turn, and we have an unforeseen path set before us.

The Wisdom of the Queen

Are you one of the millions of people worldwide who have become amateur genealogists, thanks to the amazing online tools and databases currently available? We certainly are. If you are too, then you know that sleuthing out branches of your family tree can be quite addictive.

For my birthday one year, my husband gifted me (Jackie) the services of a professional genealogical researcher. I was shocked to learn that I am related to several branches of British royalty. I was particularly surprised and delighted to learn of some family connections to the reigning monarch of Great Britain, Queen Elizabeth II.

In 2016, millions of television viewers got a fascinating, if somewhat fictionalized, glimpse of the early years of this remarkable woman via the popular Netflix miniseries *The Crown*. The series shows Elizabeth's depth of wisdom in navigating complex political matters, and though it devotes considerable time to her interest in the ministry of Billy Graham, it does not fully explore what we know to be the source of her wisdom: Elizabeth's deep and authentic faith in God.

The Oscar-winning film *The King's Speech* portrayed Britain's reluctant monarch King George VI and his battle to overcome a speech impediment in order to deliver a key radio address to the nation at the outbreak of World War II. It is a fictionalized version of very real people, challenges, and events.

Three months after that speech was successfully delivered, George VI was frantically preparing for a second critical radio address, on Christmas Eve, 1939. Radio technology was hardly two decades old, but it had already become a firmly entrenched tradition for the British monarch to deliver a Christmas Day radio address, which the BBC broadcasted throughout the vast empire. The pressure on the king to inspire, comfort, and strengthen the nation with this speech was enormous. Britain was hardly twenty-five years removed from the last devastating and costly war with Germany. Hitler's armies seemed invincible, and Britain seemed to be standing alone against the Nazi war machine. George believed himself to be ill-equipped for such a task. Yet he knew his people needed to hear from him and that his words had to be both sobering and reassuring.

As he prepared, the king's thirteen-year-old daughter, old enough to comprehend how anguished her father was about his speech, offered him a suggestion. She brought him a copy of one of her favorite poems, "God Knows," by English poet Minnie Louise Haskins. She thought its opening stanza seemed appropriate for the dark hour, the threshold of a year that could hold little good for the people of Britain. The king agreed and, at the close of his speech, read these words to the nation:

> And I said to the man who stood at the gate of the year:
> "Give me a light that I may tread safely into the
>   unknown."
> And he replied:
> "Go out into the darkness and put your hand into the
>   Hand of God.
> That shall be to you better than light and safer than a
>   known way."[6]

The message of that verse—trusting in God in a season

of fearful uncertainty—struck a deep chord and captured the imagination of the British people. It was endlessly cited and printed in the days that followed and ultimately became one of the most quoted poetic works of the twentieth century.[7] A young girl's instinct to seek comfort and guidance in the hand of a loving God was combined with a desire to point the British people to do the same.

THE LITTLE-KNOWN STORY OF QUEEN ELIZABETH

A little more than twelve years later, the same young princess who offered the idea of the famous poem to her father would be crowned Queen Elizabeth II and begin the longest reign in Britain's long, illustrious history.

That reign has seen extraordinary changes in the world and numerous crises for the British people (and more than a few family crises for the queen herself). She took the throne at the height of the Cold War and in the shadow of the threat of nuclear Armageddon. She ruled throughout the rapid and largely peaceful dissolution of the globe-spanning British Empire, in which dozens of colonial possessions in Africa and Asia achieved freedom and autonomy. She saw decades of sectarian bloodshed in Northern Ireland spill over to the streets of London in the form of terrorism. She witnessed the cultural upheavals of the late '60s and '70s, from which came the sexual revolution, the drug culture, and a widespread abandonment of Christianity and the Christian worldview. The Suez Crisis of 1956, the Falklands War, numerous recessions and financial shocks, and many other crises roiled her domain through the years.

As with all of us, her personal and family life has also not been untouched by tragedy and deep disappointment across those decades. Every mother wants to see her children doing well and succeeding at the most significant things in life, including marriage and parenting. The queen was dismayed when in

1992 she saw the world's tabloids catch fire with the news that her son Prince Andrew was separating from his wildly popular wife, Sarah "Fergie" Ferguson. Her daughter, Princess Anne, divorced her husband around that same time. Compounding the queen's pain in the midst of all the tongue wagging and gossip, a book titled *Diana: Her True Story* was published, which asserted that another son, Prince Charles, had engaged in a long-running affair and that Princess Diana, lonely and hurting, had broken their marriage vows as well. The book sold faster than the publisher could print new copies.

To cap what Elizabeth would later describe as her *annus horribilis*[8] (Latin for "horrible year"), a fire gutted a large section of Windsor Castle, doing tens of millions of dollars in damage while destroying numerous precious works of art and irreplaceable historic furnishings. The queen was reported to be devastated.

Even so, only a few days after the blaze, and in the face of all the embarrassing headlines surrounding her children, Elizabeth kept an engagement to deliver a speech at an event celebrating the fortieth anniversary of her accession to the throne. With characteristic calm and just a hint of deadpan British wit, the queen told the assembled dignitaries, "[Nineteen ninety-two] is not a year on which I shall look back with undiluted pleasure."[9]

Four years later, Queen Elizabeth would see Prince Charles's long-troubled marriage to Princess Diana end in divorce amid a never-ending hailstorm of tabloid rumors and unseemly accusations. Just twelve months after that, news of Diana's death in a late-night accident while her car was chased by a pack of paparazzi would shake the royal family, and the nation, to its foundations.

As it happened, Elizabeth had Charles and Diana's two sons, William and Harry, ages fifteen and twelve, at Balmoral Castle in Scotland for the summer at the time of the accident. In the hours and days afterward, the queen clearly made protecting and supporting the princes her overriding focus.

The crash occurred just past midnight, so the queen instructed her staff to let the children sleep. She shared the worst news they would likely ever hear when they arose the next morning. They were all scheduled to attend church that morning, and the queen's instinct was to carry on with that plan. What better place to be when heartbroken and soul-sick? However, Elizabeth asked the church leadership in advance not to directly mention the accident.

She was also deeply concerned about Diana's boys hearing or seeing disturbing details of the accident, which were being endlessly repeated on every media source in the nation. So she took the precaution of having the staff remove or disable all the televisions and radios in the residence. In those surreal days following Diana's death, Elizabeth protected the boys and their privacy with a remarkable fierceness. This choice would open her up to a firestorm of criticism and resentment from certain parts of the British media and public.

Many critics assert that the queen waited too long to make a public statement, but it is unlikely that her grandsons would agree. In a 2016 interview, Prince William expressed sincere appreciation for the way his grandmother helped him in that painful season. In the Sky News documentary, the prince revealed, "Having lost my mother at a young age, it's been particularly important to me that I've had somebody like the queen to look up to and who's been there, and who has understood some of the more complex issues when you lose a loved one."[10]

THE FAITH OF THE QUEEN

Through more than six decades of change, technological advancement, cultural upheaval, and Britain's dramatically shifting role on the world stage, Elizabeth II has carried herself with grace, dignity, and a fundamental decency that is apparent to every honest observer. At the root of this remarkable wisdom and discernment is a genuine Christian faith undergirded by a reverence for the Bible.

As the Sovereign of Great Britain, Queen Elizabeth II holds the official title Defender of the Faith and Supreme Governor of the Church of England. These titles date back to the reign of King Henry VIII. However, this queen's faith is clearly more than ceremonial.

Viewers of *The Crown* got a few glimpses of the faith of Britain's longest-reigning monarch, but nowhere near a full picture of the depth and breadth of this woman's love for God and commitment to Christ. In her Christmas address to the nation in 2002, the year she lost her mother and sister, Elizabeth shared the following: "I know just how much I rely on my faith to guide me through the good times and the bad. Each day is a new beginning. I know that the only way to live my life is to try to do what is right, to take the long view, to give of my best in all that the day brings, and to put my trust in God. . . . I draw strength from the message of hope in the Christian gospel."[11]

Two years earlier, she declared, "To many of us our beliefs are of fundamental importance. For me the teachings of Christ and my own personal accountability before God provide a framework in which I try to lead my life. I, like so many of you, have drawn great comfort in difficult times from Christ's words and example."[12]

As we write, Elizabeth remains on the throne and is arguably both the most famous woman in the world and the most popular woman in Great Britain, with approval numbers at roughly 90 percent. She is also one of the highest-profile disciples of Jesus Christ on earth.

Shortly before her coronation in 1953, Elizabeth sought the prayers of the British people. She asked them to "pray that God may give me wisdom and strength to carry out the solemn promises I shall be making, and that I may faithfully serve Him and you, all the days of my life."[13]

A prayer for wisdom. It seems that prayer was answered. Elizabeth II—a woman of legacy—has consistently exemplified the quality of Christian wisdom. And perhaps that is the greatest truth: all of us, whether we are a queen or not, can pray for a heart of wisdom to guide us through uncertain times.

Reflecting on the Roots of My Own Legacy

The story of Queen Elizabeth II and her family has always been so fascinating to me (Jackie), even before I discovered she is my ninth cousin. I was just a teenager when the televised wedding of Charles and Diana captured the imagination of the entire world. As a fifteen-year-old girl, I loved every detail of the dreamy, fairy tale–like event.

What girl doesn't enjoy tales of queens and princesses? I am no exception. I have been a voracious reader my whole life, and it is one of my favorite pastimes today. Even through the sleep-deprived years with little babies in the house, I would often read before I fell asleep, and occasionally let myself stay up for hours in the quiet of the night as a treat and immerse myself in a good story.

My favorite stories are the legacy stories of the women who came before me. My maternal grandmother—"Grannie," as we all called her—was always a big part of my life. That bond was strengthened by our attending the same church. I started singing in the church choir when I was in middle school, and my grannie was a strong alto right next to me every Sunday. It also helped that she lived a short walk away from my home. Some of my most treasured memories are of walking over to her house to help her unpack and decorate her Christmas tree each year.

Sometimes she would even let me help wrap gifts, as long as I promised not to reveal what the gifts were.

I loved hearing Grannie talk about her life growing up and the stories she heard from her mother. Grannie's mother, Frances Olivia ("Fannie"), had no memories of her own mother. She had died from complications of childbirth when Fannie was only two years old. Shortly thereafter, her father took off to dig and pan for gold in Colorado, leaving her in the care of her kindly spinster aunt, who loved her very much. Sadly, that aunt passed away when Fannie was five. So once again she found herself passed on to relatives, this time to an aunt and uncle with four young sons in Missouri. She grew up working hard to help her aunt with chores and taking care of all of those boys.

At seventeen, she wanted to marry her high school sweetheart, but her uncle refused to approve of the union. So shortly after turning eighteen, she threw her belongings out the window and climbed out to join Frank, her soon-to-be husband. After failing to find a judge in Missouri who would perform the ceremony, the couple took a train across the Kansas state line. Upon getting married, they returned to Missouri to begin their lives together.

Fannie and Frank had fourteen children, only eight of whom survived infancy. Another died at fifteen years old. My grannie was the youngest of these and lived to be ninety-two years old. At ninety, she was still driving to church every Sunday morning, swinging by to pick up her ninety-five-year-old sister on the way.

Frank was a difficult husband who was often ill. On top of this, there were many children to take care of, compounded by the grief of burying six babies and their teenage daughter. Fannie lived a hard life and lived much of it without the benefit of a strong relationship with God.

Then one summer, two of her teenage children went to a local tent revival. They came home and convinced Fannie to go with them the next night. I don't know the specifics of what happened at that meeting, but I do know that Fannie ended up living a long, fruitful life with a reputation for being a cheerful, joyful, deeply spiritual woman. I also know she was a charter member of a Pentecostal congregation and was very expressive in her praise and worship of God until the day she left this earth.

These are the stories of the women of legacy on my side of the family. One thing I have always wondered about is how Fannie managed to raise so many children who were strong believers who lived their lives with integrity and honor and in turn raised their own children who did the same. How did she come by the wisdom to become such a woman of legacy?

I am a fourth-generation Christian, and now a grandmother myself. When we gather for holidays on my side of the family, there are sixty or seventy of us, representing numerous generations. At ninety, Grannie was still hosting us all with a joyful heart, a special gift each Christmas, and unconditional love for every one of us.

What an influence her mother, that little orphaned girl, had. What a legacy she left behind! I am just one of so many who have benefitted from Fannie's choice to serve God and who have been blessed by her wisdom in passing on her love for Jesus from generation to generation. That love was first transmitted to Grannie, then to my own dear mother, and from there to me, my children, and now my grandchildren. This means I have the privilege of seeing the sixth generation of Christians in my lifetime. And I hope to live to see the seventh. What a legacy!

Today the women of our family have a getaway weekend and a quilting retreat each year at my cousin's lake home. We began the tradition of a getaway weekend about fifteen years ago, then added the family quilt retreat nine years ago. My grannie was an amazing quilter and wanted to pass down the art to the rest of us, as she had learned it from her own mother and mother-in-law. She taught me as a young girl how to crochet and showed me as a young teen how to hand quilt. Although I didn't fully appreciate it at the time, later I wanted to learn how to make a baby quilt. Shortly thereafter, we had a quilt revival in our family.

My grandmother, mother, sisters, aunts, cousins, and I participated in the first family quilt in 2009. Once a pattern was chosen, we each made twenty blocks, then swapped them so our final quilt was made up of blocks stitched by the whole family. We have gone on and made several more family quilts and many, many individual quilts, now with my five daughters having learned the art of quilting.

In my grannie's last few years, she would sit and happily volunteer to repair our mistakes with a seam ripper, sharing advice on how to make it right the next time. The gentle advice applied not only to quilting but to living our lives well, with scriptural principles lovingly passed along.

Coming together from different locations, different career paths, and different age groups, we laugh, play games, cook meals and share recipes, sew quilts, and make memories. Like every other family, we aren't perfect, but we understand the importance of passing on to the next generations the things that truly matter, like the wisdom that comes from a life of faith.

When my great-grandmother set off on the adventure of going to that tent revival with her kids so long ago, I doubt she realized the effect it would have on her life and on many who would follow her example of living a life faithful to God. I sure am grateful that she jumped in the wagon to drive to the revival and left there committed to the journey of living the rest of her life as a faithful follower of Christ.

And that's the power of wisdom. That's the power of legacy. Wisdom always sees beyond the troubles of the present and looks to the long term.

CHAPTER 5

THE LEGACY OF TEACHING

My heart is singing for joy this morning.
A miracle has happened! The light of
understanding has shone upon my little
pupil's mind, and behold, all things are
changed.

—Anne Sullivan, tutor of Helen Keller[1]

When we think of legacy, one of the first places we go is to our teachers—women who have left an imprint in our lives. Perhaps one little-known story that deserves our attention is the story of Huldah. Her teaching of Scripture to the king helped change the course of a nation.

A Nation Gone Wayward

It is a dark time in the nation of Judah. Amon was king of Judah for just two short years before being assassinated in his own house. His son, Josiah, must assume the throne at just eight years of age.

His own father and grandfather led the kingdom's headlong plunge into a pit of paganism. Worship of Jehovah has become a rarity in the land. Solomon's formerly magnificent temple has fallen into disuse and disrepair, even as "high places" for the worship of demon-deities like Ashtoreth, Dagon, Molech, and

Baal have emerged all over the country like cancerous growths. These sites for pagan sacrifice and acts of unspeakable immorality attract steady streams of devotees from among the citizens of Judah. Josiah's grandfather even introduced elements of this idol worship into the holy temple.

Into the midst of this darkness the young king steps, with righteous intentions but precious little light to show him how to return the nation to God, or what that even looks like. He begins by ordering repairs and restoration for the neglected temple of Solomon. This includes removing the defiling pagan features added by his grandfather.

It is in the midst of this work that the discovery is made. In the catacombs beneath the temple complex, in a dusty secret room that once held the temple's treasures of gold and jewels, workmen find an even greater treasure: an ancient scroll of forgotten knowledge. This is reported to the high priest, Hilkiah, who carefully transports the document directly to the king.

What he is carrying is a copy of the fifth and final book of Moses, which will be known to future generations as Deuteronomy. It is sadly telling that this is the first time either man has ever laid eyes on any portion of the Word of God. So out of touch with her spiritual roots has Judah become that not even the high priest himself has ever read a single word of the Law of Moses.

Josiah commands that the scroll be read to him, and this leads to his undoing. As the document is read, the king hears for the first time, in starkly specific terms, what God asked of His people as they entered the land of promise. For the first time in his life, Josiah hears the extraordinary blessings that will flow to them as a people if they will remain faithful to the One who delivered them from bondage. He hears the litany of horrific curses that will fall on them if they abandon worship of the one true God and follow after idols.

In the pure light of the sacred Scriptures, an understanding of the enormity of Judah's infidelity to her God hits Josiah like a tsunami. A wave of dread washes over him as he takes in the faithless depravity of the nation under his stewardship. Surely, the cup of God's wrathful judgment is brimming full by now.

WHO WILL TEACH GOD'S WORD?

Josiah issues a simple plea: "Go and inquire of the LORD for me and for the people and for all Judah about what is written in this book that has been found" (2 Kings 22:13). Josiah needs someone who knows God's ways and the meaning of these sacred writings. He needs a wise teacher who can guide him. Clearly, Hilkiah the high priest is not the person for the job. He is almost as much in the dark about the Bible as Josiah.

Here the Scriptures seem to offer a divine pause. While Hilkiah is not the right person, he leads a delegation to the doorstep of Huldah. Huldah is described as a prophetess (2 Kings 22:14). She knows God's Word and she teaches it.

It's fascinating that in this time of trouble, the leaders of Judah knew exactly the address of the person with wisdom. Isn't that interesting? Huldah is mentioned only briefly in Scripture. She held no high office. She had no advanced social status or great wealth. Her husband helped keep the king's wardrobe. Yet when the people needed a source for wisdom, they knew precisely where to find it.

There's a simple message to us all. If we cultivate a heart of wisdom, even if it doesn't occupy the stage, it will always be recognized by people around us.

Huldah's words—her teachings—serve as encouragement to Josiah. Although Huldah prophesies that God will bring disaster to Judah, she assures the leaders that since Josiah has been responsive to God, this judgment will not take place during his lifetime. Spurred by this powerful prophecy, Josiah goes on to lead a crucial but short-lived revival in Judah. Armed with the knowledge of the Word, Josiah pulls down the high places and revitalizes worship of Jehovah God in the temple, in accordance with the once-forgotten Levitical guidelines.

In the centuries to come, the rabbinic literature will name Huldah as one of the seven great prophetesses of Israel, alongside Sarah, Miriam, Deborah, Hannah, Abigail, and Esther. That is extraordinary company. And Huldah's story should serve as the greatest encouragement for our own souls. If we cultivate a heart of wisdom, a heart willing to teach, we can impact a nation.

The Teachers of Our Own Lives

Few activities carry more power to create a lasting legacy in this world than teaching. And like Huldah of old, women today are fully equipped by God to transmit truth and wisdom in a way that shapes culture.

EARLY IMPACT

Who among us hasn't been profoundly influenced by a gifted teacher at some point early in life? For me (Jackie), that unforgettable teacher was Mrs. Hughes.

In my home church where I grew up, there were quite a few teachers from my public school who also taught Bible lessons at church on Sundays. One of the most popular of these was Mrs. Hughes. I couldn't wait to be old enough to hear Mrs. Hughes tell the Bible stories in our children's service. She brought the stories to life each week and left us with a cliffhanger ending every time.

Finally, just before my fifth birthday, I got to move up to the multi-aged class that Mrs. Hughes taught. I remember her telling us the story of Joseph's life over several weeks. When I realized these weren't just stories but true events recorded in the Bible, I was enthralled on one hand and convicted on the other. I wanted to live my life for Jesus, but I didn't want to have to go through trials like Joseph. Early on, I made the decision to live my life according to the principles taught from the Bible by Mrs. Hughes—and by my parents, who lived them out before me every day.

TEACHER OF MORE THAN SCHOOL LESSONS

For me (Lauren), well, the teacher I credit for launching my academic and spiritual journeys is the person cowriting this book with me—my mom, Jackie. You see, I was homeschooled through the eighth grade.

My mom was a thorough and effective teacher, and I'm so grateful for her commitment to my academic life. But even more than that, there are valuable lessons children learn from their mothers in day-to-day activities. Many of the things that have influenced me were not what my mother taught me through my formal education but rather what she lived out moment by moment. She certainly taught me English, history, and science, but she also taught me commitment, selflessness, and respect.

My mother will tell you that she felt ill-equipped to teach. As with many moms who contemplate teaching, it is easy to equate being *uncredentialed* with being *unqualified*. This is a mistake. For me and my siblings who started our education at Mom's kitchen table, the results speak for themselves.

I went on to earn an undergraduate degree in classics and two master's degrees, a master of arts in pastoral counseling and a master of arts in theological studies. And as I write, I am earning a PhD in ethics and public policy, with an emphasis in leadership. I think Mom did okay, don't you?

Of course, I also owe a huge debt to my mother for the *spiritual* lessons I learned from her. As is the case with most children blessed to be born to godly, Bible-honoring mothers, my first glimmers of insight about the love of God and the redeeming work of Jesus Christ came at her knee. My parents raised us in church, but their faith went well beyond the church walls. At home, I remember seeing my parents read their Bibles daily. I was impacted by seeing my mom and dad live out their faith. I remember my mom practicing Scripture memorization with me and my siblings and praying passages of the Psalms at night before we were tucked in bed. Her daily influence truly left its mark on my life. Christian mothers are the most powerful and important teachers in all the world.

Christian history is filled with women, like Mrs. Hughes, who understood and championed the destiny-altering, culture-shaping power of teaching. And few have championed this cause with more passion or left a bigger legacy than a certain poor girl born on a Massachusetts farm in 1797.

The Teaching Legacy of Mary Lyon

Today while I (Lauren) am pursuing my PhD, it is easy to take for granted the potential that women have to pursue higher education. That has not always been the case. When I think of the story of Mary Lyon, I'm aware that women of today owe a debt to trailblazers like her.

On a crisp autumn day in 1837, scores of young women began arriving by horse and carriage at a large, freshly painted building in South Hadley, Massachusetts. Some had traveled for days to reach this destination. By day's end, eighty such girls had gathered to make up the inaugural class of the Mount Holyoke Female Seminary (later renamed Mount Holyoke College). They came to do something precious few women in America had ever received the opportunity to do: pursue a degree in higher education.

Although the United States of America was still quite young at this time, the nation already had 120 colleges for men. On that fall day, Mount Holyoke became the first for women. These newly arrived students were giddy and nervous. In addition to their clothing, bedding, and grooming necessities, they had been instructed to bring an atlas, a dictionary, and, very importantly, a Bible.

Mary Lyon, just forty years old, was the visionary force behind Holyoke. For years, she had carried a burning belief that women needed and deserved a complete Christian education and that a just and godly society would maximize the potential of girls. She envisioned a place in which young women could be enriched and equipped in both mind and spirit. So she chose as the new college's motto a phrase from Psalm 144:

> That our daughters may be as corner stones,
> polished after the similitude of a palace.
>
> —Psalm 144:12 KJV

While this college for women was the culmination of a lifelong dream, countless hours of fervent prayer, and extraordinary effort, it began with an unlikely start.

THE BEGINNING OF THE DREAM

Mary was one of seven poor children raised by a pioneering farmer in northwestern Massachusetts. As people of strong faith, Mary's parents made sure their entire family made the two-mile trek to the nearest Methodist church every Sunday. All made the trip on foot except for Mary's mother and youngest sibling, who sat on the family's only horse.

A rigorous life became a battle for survival when Mary's father died suddenly when Mary was only five. Her mother and the older siblings were left to try to run the farm. Eventually, her mother remarried and bore additional children.

However, when Mary was only thirteen, Mary's mother was pressured by her new husband to move to another town and leave her children from her first marriage behind, which she did. In our day, a thirteen-year-old girl might be taking her first babysitting job or maybe even just struggling to straighten up her room every day and keep up with schoolwork. Imagine the burden on a young Mary, running the household for an older brother as he attempted to scratch an existence out of the rocky soil of the hundred-acre farm. This meant days filled with cooking on the open-hearth fire, preserving summer vegetables and fruits, curing meat, churning butter, baking bread, spinning and weaving wool, sewing garments, making soap and candles, hand-washing clothes, and doing countless other chores required of a pioneer homemaker.

Because of these duties, she had to forgo much of the minimal education offered to girls in that place and time. But Mary was intelligent and hungry to learn. At every opportunity, she found ways to grab an education in bits and pieces as she grew to adulthood. As a young adult, she found herself alternating between learning and teaching.

One of those teaching jobs put her under the leadership of Reverend Joseph Emerson, a pioneer in American Christian education. Under Emerson's mentorship, Mary saw firsthand how her two driving passions—her love for God and her love for advanced learning—could combine to equip young people to do great things. Soon she had a vision for a place that would give young women the opportunity she never had. This would be a place where women would maximize their potential and be challenged and enriched in mind, body, and spirit.

LIVING OUT THE VISION

Once this vision was fully formed in her mind and articulated on paper, Mary began the seemingly impossible quest of bringing her dream to reality. Her first stop was the office of the heads of the Congregationalist denomination to which she belonged. She knew that her church had in recent years fully funded the establishment of numerous four-year colleges for men. She was hopeful that the leadership would see the value and wisdom of funding at least one college for women, especially since it would be the very first of its kind in the young, rapidly growing United States. They did not agree with her vision.

Undaunted, Mary began funding her dream the hard way, one modest donation at a time. She knocked on doors of Christian businessmen, friends, colleagues, acquaintances, and essentially anyone who would sit still long enough to hear her sales pitch. Apparently, it was quite a presentation. People who heard it described it as fast-paced, passionate, fact-filled, and compelling. Mary was prepared to overcome every objection and wear down the sympathetic but reluctant. Finally, after three years of relentless fundraising, she had accumulated the fifteen thousand dollars she needed to begin. There had been a few large donations of a thousand dollars or more along the way, but most of that staggering sum came in contributions of five dollars and ten dollars from families of modest means. Many of these families had beloved daughters they hoped could attend such a college someday. And many of their daughters ultimately did.

After spending several years raising donor awareness for the Museum of the Bible project, we feel an extra measure of respect for what Mary accomplished. Like Mary, we began with a handful of donors and worked hard to find others. Now we have more than fifty thousand! We know the effort takes perseverance. Mary's accomplishment is all the more impressive given the day and culture in which she lived. We may be separated in time by 180 years, yet we can identify with having a God-given dream and struggling to bring it to reality. Mary saw her vision through to its fulfillment.

Land was purchased in South Hadley, Massachusetts, and a building constructed. Then came the decision about what to call the school. Supporters and well-wishers believed it should bear Mary's name, as it owed its existence almost exclusively to the sheer force of Mary's iron will and boundless energy. She would not hear of it. Instead she adopted the name of a nearby geological feature, and the dream of Mount Holyoke Female Seminary came true.

True to Mary's vision, the school provided a rigorous education that included not only a slate of arts and literature but also high-level mathematics and science. In addition, the curriculum emphasized physical fitness, something virtually unheard of for women at that time.

She hired a first-rate faculty and taught some subjects herself, including the Bible. Many of her students would later recall her powerful gift for bringing the Word of God to life. A journal entry of one early Holyoke student records, "I have just been looking up the passages which were read to us this morning from Miss Lyon's Bible; and when she reads to us, it always seems to me that there are treasures in her Bible that were left out of mine. But as usual I have found all, and here they are."[2]

THE LASTING LEGACY OF MARY LYON

Mary Lyon's legacy is hard to overstate. Having blazed the trail and broken the barrier, Mount Holyoke College became the model for other great women's colleges that followed. It is the eldest sibling among the Seven Sisters, a group of historic and prestigious women's colleges in the northeast that also includes Barnard, Bryn Mawr, Smith, Wellesley, Vassar, and Radcliffe.

Over its nearly two-hundred-year history, the institution has produced many noteworthy graduates who have made the world better in innumerable ways. One of the first graduates of Mount Holyoke, and therefore one of the first women to earn a college degree on American soil, was Lucy Stone. Stone went on to become a leading abolitionist, championing the cause to end the scourge of slavery in this nation in an era in which it was rare for a woman to take such a high-profile role in a cause. The same is true for Mount Holyoke graduate Helen Pitts Douglass (class of 1859), who was a powerful voice for ending slavery and became the second wife of abolitionist icon Frederick Douglass.

One of the earliest advocates for women's suffrage, Olympia Brown, was a Mount Holyoke graduate. She lived long enough to be able, at the age of eighty-five, to cast her very first vote after the passage of the Nineteenth Amendment to the Constitution. The poet Emily Dickinson attended Mount Holyoke, as did the nineteenth-century novelist Mary E. Wilkins Freeman.

What is more, the strong emphasis on science and mathematics that Mary insisted on building into her college's curriculum resulted in many prominent scientists, physicians, and researchers flowing into the American stream of progress. Among these are:

- Dr. Dorothy Hansine Andersen, the first person to identify and describe cystic fibrosis, opening the door for research and treatment
- Dr. Virginia Apgar, the pioneering obstetrician who lent her name to the Apgar score, used today to assess the health of newborn infants
- Rachel Fuller Brown, a chemist who co-developed the first useful antifungal antibiotic
- Helen Sawyer Hogg, an astronomer noted for groundbreaking research into globular clusters and variable stars

And thousands of others in every realm of endeavor. That is an amazing legacy, particularly for a woman with such an unlikely start in life. But then that is the way of our God. Mary was mindful of this. About a year before Mount Holyoke opened its doors, Mary had participated in the laying of the cornerstone for that very first structure. On that stone she had written, "The Lord hath remembered our low estate," a reference to Luke 1:48, wherein her namesake, the virgin Mary, offers up her "Magnificat," a song of praise to God for allowing her, a poor rural girl, to give birth to something wonderful. At that same ceremony, Mary is reported to have said in genuine humility, "The feeble efforts which I am permitted to put forth in cooperating with others in laying the foundation of this new seminary will probably do more for the cause of Christ, after I am laid in my grave, than all I have done in my life before."[3]

This is how a woman of legacy thinks. She takes the long view, with her sights set on the future. She sees generations yet unborn. We can all take heart from Mary Lyon's story. She faced deep hurt when her mother left her, and the struggles of daily living prevented her from pursuing her own education. When the time came for her to launch the dream of higher education for women, she didn't let the naysayers or her unfavorable circumstances stop her. Eighteen decades later, the school to which she gave birth is still going strong, with an endowment of more than $667 million.

Teaching—transmitting knowledge, truth, insight, and values—is a powerful way to shape the members of the next generation and set them up for their own far-reaching influence.

Discovering Your Teaching Legacy

As we've seen, at a certain point in her life Mary Lyon would have seemed the unlikeliest of candidates for creating a world-changing teaching legacy. As we write these words, we are excited to think of how many other women have a similar gift waiting to come alive. Whether you teach by vocation, lead a children's Sunday school class, or simply make an effort to share truth with your peers, there is no end to the possibilities of how you can pass on a legacy through teaching.

When a willing heart yields to the hand of God, unlikely things become commonplace. As the prophet Samuel told a father of several sons when on his quest to find God's choice for the next king of Israel, "The LORD doesn't see things the way you see them. People judge by outward appearance, but the LORD looks at the heart" (1 Sam. 16:7 NLT).

THE UNLIKELY START TO A TEACHING LEGACY

If you were searching for a person to launch a global Bible study movement, one who would help millions around the world gain a better understanding of God's Word, you would probably never consider a woman matching this description:

- Divorced nurse in her late twenties with two children
- Rebellious and running from God
- Had a series of bad choices in men and unhealthy relationships, including a husband who committed suicide and a two-year affair with a married man

Nevertheless, according to her own testimony, in 1963 all of this was true of one of our greatest living Bible teachers—Kay Arthur.

Although going to church with her family was an integral part of Kay's childhood, the Bible played no role in her life. She wasn't encouraged to read or study it. She found it boring and irrelevant. Kay had a religion without a relationship. But all that changed when on July 16, 1963, unable to stop being immoral after her divorce, she fell to her knees and cried out, "God, I don't care what You do to me. I don't care if I never see another man as long as I live. I don't care what You do to my two boys. I don't care if You paralyze me from the neck down, if You'll just give me peace."[4]

Kay was twenty-nine when God gave her the Prince of Peace, the Lord Jesus Christ. With Jesus came a hunger for the Word of God. Ironically, several days later a young man gave Kay a modern translation of the New Testament. One of the first Scriptures she read was Romans 9:25, which Kay recalls as saying, "He called her beloved when there was nothing lovely about her."

GOD TRAINS YOU FOR HIS PURPOSE

A few years after her salvation experience, Kay met and married Jack Arthur, a man of integrity and a seasoned missionary. To join Jack in his mission work in Mexico, Kay sold everything she had and moved with her two sons to Guadalajara, Mexico. Little did they realize God had a ministry far more expansive than Mexico, but first Kay needed to learn how to study God's Word.

When their fellow missionaries in language school pleaded for someone to work with their teens and no one responded, Kay told the Lord she would do it if He would tell her how. He made it clear: the teens needed to know God's Word for themselves. During the next three and half years, God laid the foundation for what, in His sovereignty, was to become a worldwide ministry of establishing people in God's Word.

When health problems forced the Arthurs to return to Tennessee in the late 1960s, Kay would discover that God had a greater plan than hers. They moved to Chattanooga, where Jack was hired to build and manage a Christian radio station. At the request of a local pastor and his wife, Kay started teaching a Bible study for teenagers in her home. The study had simple beginnings (Kay's podium in her living room was the high chair of her third son, David!), but it expanded in size and scope so rapidly that soon she and Jack were looking for larger places to meet. Although it was the late sixties, the days of "hippie coffee house ministries," God impressed on Kay's and Jack's hearts that He wanted them to meet on a farm. In 1970, they bought a thirty-two-acre farm with two barns, and Kay started holding the Bible studies there. In a short amount of time, large numbers of college students and adults were learning how to read and study the Bible for themselves. It soon became clear to both Kay and Jack that they had a bona fide, God-ordained ministry on their hands, and Precept Ministries was born.

CULTIVATING THE GIFT

Kay Arthur's unique approach involved far more than simply developing study curricula for the various books of the Bible. She, with the help of others from their ministry, systematized a way to study the Bible inductively. The inductive method is a simple three-step process of (1) making observations about the text, (2) interpreting what the text says, and (3) applying the text to daily life. Anyone who learned her method could experience a lifetime of mining the unfathomable riches of God's Word.

God continued opening doors for Kay and Jack: radio in 1978, television in 1981, and books and devotionals written along the way—all with God's Word front and center. With these new teaching outlets came invitations to teach at conferences. Then in the summer of 1983, God launched the ministry internationally into Mexico, Guatemala, Korea, Romania, and Russia. Today Precept Ministries teaches and trains Bible study leaders in 180 countries, and Kay's Bible studies have been translated into seventy languages. Kay has written more than one hundred books and Bible studies, with more than eleven million currently in print. As you read these words, Precept's Inductive Bible Study groups regularly gather in all fifty states of the USA. And Kay's radio program is heard on more than one thousand radio stations around the world.

What began as a simple living room Bible study for teens has now become Precept Ministries International, which spans the globe and has touched untold millions. Today Kay says about her ministry, "Only God, in His sovereignty, could do this. If you knew our backgrounds, our lack of education and training, you would understand Jack and I certainly were not capable of doing it ourselves. This is the Lord's doing!"

And that's perhaps the greatest message of Huldah, Mary Lyon, and Kay Arthur: you don't have to have all the degrees, the background, or the training to become a great teacher. It starts with faith and a desire to learn, which often bubbles over into a desire to teach others. That's the common denominator of each of these three women—faith, a desire to learn, and a desire to teach others. We don't need to make it more complicated than that.

Some of the most effective and innovative Bible teachers today are women. Beth Moore, Priscilla Shirer, Lisa Bevere, Lysa TerKeurst, Raechel Myers, Amanda Bible Williams, and so many others teach with authority and effectiveness on global platforms. We love seeing how these women and others—though none of them claim to be or could be perfect—have been so effective in expanding the kingdom of God.

Of course, it isn't just Bible teachers and women in full-time ministry building legacies through the power of teaching. Countless women in educational settings, in the corporate world, and in their homes are impacting the world and improving the future through their willingness to teach.

There is an old saying that asserts, "A good teacher is like a candle—it consumes itself to light the way for others." There is truth in that statement. No matter what the context—school, church, home, or business—the woman who chooses to teach gives of herself sacrificially, but the light of that sacrifice illuminates the future.

When I (Lauren) think about lighting the way for others, I

think about my sisters. One of my sisters, Lindy, has served as a social worker in the adoption and foster care system, teaching young moms and families about parenting, trauma, and basic life skills. She's an inspiration to me and an example of how the gift of teaching can be employed in every environment.

My sister Danielle teaches others using her artistic abilities. In each masterpiece she creates, there are biblical themes woven throughout for observers to discover. She is a part of the team that oversees the Museum of the Bible social media, where she uses her gifts creatively to communicate the Bible to potentially millions.

As a mother, a mother-in-law, and a grandmother, I (Jackie) want to encourage the young women in my family, as well as others who come across my path, "Whatever you do, do it all for the glory of God" (1 Cor. 10:31). My girls all have different strengths and gifts, as does every woman on this planet. I want them to feel empowered to be whatever they are called and inspired to be, and to light the way for future generations. The key to being a light is letting God shine bright within you.

The gift of lighting the way for others is a powerful culture changer and an opportunity for us to make change happen wherever we are—in our homes, our churches, our neighborhoods, and beyond.

Maybe you don't think of yourself as a teacher, but we all have strengths to offer. What are your strong points? How can you share one of those with someone else? Maybe the new staffer in your office needs help with the printer. Or you could show a new bride how to cook a homemade meal. The kid next door might enjoy learning how to plant flowers. The teenage boy could use a hand finding books in the library. Whatever your skill set is, your world is full of rich opportunities. Think of that: God is calling *you* to join the ranks of light bearers today. What's more, He has fully equipped you to shine.

CHAPTER 6

THE LEGACY OF RESCUE

*Throughout history, in the dark night of need,
God awakens ordinary people to the torrent
of His love, shattering the silence and fueling
in their hearts an unquenchable desire to
spread the love they've found to the broken
and discarded.*

—Louie Giglio[1]

Some of the top-grossing movies of our time—like *The Hunger Games* or *The Avengers*—involve elements of danger, intrigue, and rescue. Rescue captures the idea of living for a noble cause, something bigger than yourself. Every day, women around this country and around the world hold back the tide of evil and save people around them with acts both great and small. In our look at the history of faithful women, we see where one of those acts saved a king.

The Incredible Rescue of a King

She carries a blanket-wrapped bundle through the hallways of the Jerusalem palace. She prays they won't be seen or heard. Detection will mean certain death—for her and the infant hidden within her blanket. And although Jehosheba does not know it, hanging in the balance is nothing less than God's plan to save the world.

Please don't cry, little one. Not now.

The tiny, precious cargo has a name. Joash is the rightful heir to the throne of Israel. He is the only living male descendant in the royal line of King David of the tribe of Judah.

His grandmother has massacred his father and the rest of the royal family. She is an evil, idolatrous woman whose father was wicked Ahab of the Northern Kingdom. She seeks the throne for herself. She wants to reign just like her mother, Jezebel, and continue to lead the nation in idolatry and the worship of Baal.

In the face of this murderer, what would you do? Would you save your own life? Jehosheba is the boy's aunt, and her name means "the Lord is a promise keeper." She is of the royal blood of David too, and she is also the wife of the high priest. Jehosheba knows that there is one child that the power-hungry grandmother has missed—Joash. So at the risk of her own life, she slips Joash out of the royal residence and hides him away in the nearby temple built by her ancestor, Solomon, son of David.

Much more hangs in the balance than just this one baby. It is a family's legacy. Joash is part of an ancient prophetic promise concerning the future Savior of the world. More than a thousand years earlier, this infant's forefather Jacob had prophesied that "The scepter will not depart from Judah, nor the ruler's staff from between his feet, until he comes to whom it belongs" (Gen. 49:10 NET). The "He" to whom the kingly scepter truly belongs is the promised Messiah. Joash is part of this Davidic line of kings that will lead to the ultimate Redeemer-King. The scarlet thread of redemption that has run through history since God promised Eve that one day her "seed"—her offspring—would crush the head of the serpent (Gen. 3:15) includes the bloodline of Joash, continuing to a stable in Bethlehem and on to a cross-topped hill outside Jerusalem.

Without the benefit of foresight, Jehosheba can't know all that she holds in her hands. Perhaps she only grasps the fear of the moment, fear for her own life and the life of the child. But in a moment of compassion—in a moment of rescue—she acts.

And that is the call to all women everywhere: act on your heart of compassion. Act in the moment when God nudges you to act, to rescue. God has uniquely equipped women to sense the need of the hour, the need of the heart, and to step in and to save. In many cases, we'll never know the full impact of those actions.

Joash will be hidden, nurtured, and taught the ways of God for more than six years. When it is safe, he will emerge as the rightful child-king of Judah, and his grandmother, with all her wicked ways, will be removed from the throne. For all time, Joash will be remembered as one of the good kings of Judah. And more than eight centuries later, a descendant will be born. He will be called Immanuel, meaning "God with us." It will be possible because a brave woman with a heart to rescue the innocent risked everything.

LOOKING FOR WAYS TO RESCUE

Let's pause for a moment. We know there are people who are vulnerable all around us, many of whom are unsafe even in the womb. We know that each unborn child is loved by God and that abortion is a sad reality of our time. For those reading these words, we can all be reminded to be attentive to the opportunities around us to provide rescue for someone—perhaps a neighbor, a single mom, a destitute family, children needing foster care, or an orphan in need of a forever family. We love the wisdom of the book of Proverbs, which commands us, "Deliver those who are being taken away to death, and those who are staggering to slaughter, oh hold them back" (Prov. 24:11 NASB).

On a personal level, I (Lauren) am encouraged that I see women my age who are taking up the call to rescue. I think about Lila Rose, who is working heroically to save the lives of the unborn. My mom and I met Lila at an event a couple of years ago and have stayed in touch with this courageous woman ever since. I've loved getting to know Lila and her fierce passion for the most vulnerable: children in the womb. We recently had the chance to meet up in Washington, D.C., and chat over hot tea. As we sipped our tea and ate a scone or two (or three!), Lila spoke with unforgettable conviction about her work. Lila is the founder of Live Action, a pro-life human rights organization that seeks to end abortion and bring respect for all human life. She cares deeply about people in every stage of life. Despite her youth and her sometimes unpopular position, she's had incredible opportunities to speak on behalf of life, appearing on *Tucker Carlson Tonight*, *CNN*, *HLN*, and other national shows. Also most major news outlets, including the *Los Angeles Times*, the *Washington Post*, CBS, and *ABC Nightline* have featured her investigative reporting.

For me (Jackie), it seems that God is so often speaking to us about the idea of rescue. As a family, we enjoy and appreciate modern, contemporary worship music, but we also have a special place in our hearts for the classic hymns of the church. One that we find particularly meaningful is a great anthem by Fanny Crosby, written after visiting a mission shelter for the poor in one of the troubled sections of New York City. Crosby returned home and immediately wrote a hymn with the following familiar chorus:

> Rescue the perishing, care for the dying,
> Jesus is merciful, Jesus will save.[2]

I grew up singing this as well as other Fanny Crosby hymns in the church choir, next to my grandmother, with my mother playing the piano and her cousin directing the choir. (We will explore the legacy of this remarkable hymn writer in chapter 9.) Fanny knew, as we do, that without a doubt one of the core mandates for the people of God is to rescue the perishing. This extends far beyond championing the unborn. Our call to be rescuers must certainly extend to people who are victims of modern-day slavery. These people have not lost their lives, but they have lost something precious—their freedom.

People who are bravely battling involuntary servitude in our day can take inspiration from the selfless courage of one woman whose life story reads like a Hollywood adventure thriller.

The Legacy of Rescue Begins with Hope

In 1822, Harriet Tubman was born into slavery. Like many slaves in that era, she was never exactly sure of her birthday, but she was sure about her relationship with God through Christ.

She attended church services at a nearby Methodist church. There she dedicated her life to God at an early age. Despite being beaten and whipped numerous times throughout her childhood, she kept the hope that she would one day escape. With that hope, she said plainly, "Liberty or death—one or the other, I mean to have."[3] As a Christian, she knew that either outcome would result in freedom.

In 1849, around the age of twenty-seven, Tubman made good on her vow and fled to Philadelphia, 150 miles to the north. However, she could not enjoy her newfound freedom knowing that so many relatives and loved ones remained in bondage back in Maryland. She immediately began leading rescue parties back to eastern Maryland. Tubman made six such heroic missions into Maryland. She believed the Spirit of God guided and helped her as she carried out these incredibly dangerous rescues, instructing her about which routes to take, where to hide, and when to keep moving. The people she led safely to freedom believed it too. She took pride in saying she "never lost a passenger."[4]

She continued to guide groups of fleeing slaves northward into Canada via the Underground Railroad until the outbreak of the Civil War. At that point, she attached herself to the Union Army, first working as a cook and a nurse, and eventually as an armed scout and spy. Tubman soon became the first woman to lead an armed expedition in that conflict. She guided the famous raid at Combahee Ferry, resulting in the liberation of more than seven hundred slaves.

The people she rescued called her "Moses," for obvious reasons. Yet her commitment to helping the oppressed continued long after slavery as an institution ended in this nation. Tubman founded a home in Auburn, New York, to care for elderly and sick people without families. Virtually penniless, she spent her final years as a resident in one of the very homes she had established years earlier. She died in 1913 at the age of ninety-two, poor yet with a rich legacy of people she had rescued.

THE LIVING LEGACY OF RESCUE

It is easy to read these words and consider Harriet Tubman's legacy finished, a thing of the past, yet it lives on in remarkable, undeniable ways. After emancipation and the Civil War, many of the families and individuals rescued by Tubman over the years settled in the community of Auburn in upstate New York, and today you'll find Harriet Tubman's legacy residing all over the northeast United States and eastern Canada. It is quite literally a living legacy. The descendants of slaves she rescued and led to freedom number in the thousands.

One such descendant, Tina Wyatt, attended the March 2017 opening of the Harriet Tubman Underground Railroad National Historic Park Visitor Center. The historic visitor center is located on the grounds of Blackwater Wildlife Refuge in Cambridge, Maryland. That overcast spring day, Wyatt stood at the edge of the swamp, looking out over the labyrinth of salty tidal wetlands, marshes, rivers, dense forests, and a few open fields. She thought of her great-grandmother, Anna Marie Stewart, who generations ago trudged through that very swamp on her way to freedom. Stewart had been picked up by one of Tubman's rescue parties, and she followed them through snake-infested lands under the cover of darkness until they reached the safety of the north. Because of Tubman's commitment to rescuing fellow slaves and because of Stewart's willingness to risk everything to escape bondage, Wyatt could stand on the edge of the swamp 150 years later as a free woman.

Tubman to Stewart to Wyatt. Wyatt was just one of several descendants of these rescued individuals in attendance to witness the opening of the visitor center. That is the power of the legacy of rescue. Tubman never saw the thousands of descendants whose lives she was changing, yet today they live on as a monument to her boldness. Sometimes God gives us a glimpse of the impact of our rescue. And sometimes, although we may never see the influence we have on other people's lives, their descendants will, and they will thank us for it.

The impulse to be free seems to be hardwired into the human soul. God never intended for one human to dominate or own another. Sadly, after the fall of mankind, slavery spread across the planet like a virus. Just as slavery was not present before the fall, it will not be present at the end, and in Christ its injustice will be set right. Whenever we reject God, enslavement and bondage arise. The liberating power that Jesus Christ unleashed on the world in the first century has proven to be the most potent force the world has ever seen for rescue.

Jesus cited this as a central part of His mission when He chose to read a passage from chapter 61 of Isaiah in a synagogue one day:

> The Spirit of the LORD is upon Me,
> Because He has anointed Me

To preach the gospel to the poor;
He has sent Me to heal the brokenhearted,
To proclaim liberty to the captives
And recovery of sight to the blind,
To set at liberty those who are oppressed;
To proclaim the acceptable year of the LORD.

—Luke 4:18–19 NKJV

When Moses rejected his adoptive Egyptian identity, embraced his Hebrew lineage, and received God's command to free the Israelites, the idea of slavery became repulsive to him. And the end of institutionalized slavery in the English-speaking world began, in large part, through the preaching and campaigning of individuals such as William Wilberforce, Hannah More, and other like-minded Christians in Great Britain. We know that Wilberforce's view of slavery as an extreme evil to be eradicated from civilization came into focus only after he became a committed Christian. Then, as now, it seems to be the people who know God's heart best who despise slavery most.

THE FIGHT FOR RESCUE CONTINUES TODAY

While some people may view slavery as an artifact of history, it remains alive and well in our world today.

On the eve of the Civil War, the total slave population in the United States was roughly four million souls.[5] An appalling number to consider. Nevertheless, conservative estimates suggest that today there are somewhere between twenty million and thirty million enslaved individuals in the world.[6] The majority of these people suffer in developing or totalitarian nations, with no hope of having a life they can call their own. It is a shocking fact, however, that as many as sixty thousand people in the United States are effectively owned by someone else.[7] This ought not be so in a place described as the land of the free.

Slavery in the US looks different now than it did 150 years ago, but it still exists. Today it is commonly called human trafficking. Traffickers sometimes lure immigrants to the US under the promise of a better job. When this "better job" turns out to be forced labor, the immigrants feel they can't leave, since the traffickers often charge exorbitant travel fees or withhold work visas to keep the immigrants dependent. Slavery also happens to people born in the United States. Teens who have run away from home can be picked up by a trafficker (or pimp) and forced or coerced into prostitution. Or a man who poses as a boyfriend turns out to be a trafficker, forcing a woman into prostitution and threatening her and her family if she tries to leave. And sadly, sometimes a child's own family members will sell the child for sexual exploitation. However slavery occurs, the result is a person who needs to be rescued.

Worldwide, modern-day slavery exists in several forms, including forced labor, bonded labor, involuntary domestic servitude, the abduction of children for use as soldiers, and sexual slavery. Of course, all forms of human bondage are an abomination and antithetical to the revelation of God's character given to us in Jesus Christ. However, sexual slavery and the human trafficking machinery that feeds this monster's insatiable appetite represent an especially dark form of the world's oldest and vilest institution.

Fortunately, we have many Harriet Tubmans among us in our day. One of those is a fierce campaigner against the global cancer of human trafficking, and a relentless advocate for many of the most oppressed and vulnerable girls on earth. And she is building an extraordinary legacy one rescue at a time.

The Legacy of Rescue Begins with Seeing

In 2006, during her many travels, Christine Caine, Australian-born and of Greek heritage, walked through the airport in

Thessaloniki, Greece. She saw a series of handmade posters for missing girls, which troubled her. She inquired further and found that these girls were the victims of human trafficking. Seeing those posters set Christine on a path of liberation efforts in the mode of Jehosheba, Tubman, and Wilberforce.

In 2008, Christine and her husband founded A21 with a shockingly bold mission: "To abolish slavery everywhere, forever." A21's vision statement is equally audacious: "Freedom. That's our goal for every human being on the planet." They also founded Equip & Empower Ministries, which focuses on biblical teaching, training, and equipping for local churches and individual believers.

Christine's organization attacks the beast of modern slavery on three fronts through a strategy she calls "Reach, Rescue, and Restore." This involves reaching vulnerable girls in key areas and educating them about the deceptive tactics and methods of the traffickers before they can fall prey to them. Members of the organization work with local, national, and international law enforcement to rescue enslaved girls, assist in the prosecution of traffickers, and collaborate with governments and other NGOs to eradicate slavery at every level.

The restoring happens through a network of safe houses and centers where, in addition to shelter, rescued girls receive love, ministry, medical treatment, counseling, education, employment training, and much more. The restoration program is designed around the individual needs of each unique and precious girl. This "aftercare," as Christine calls it, results in some extraordinary transformations.

It is heartbreaking to see the physical damage sexual slavery does to girls. Broken teeth, scars, burn marks, drug addiction, malnutrition, and of course sexually transmitted diseases are common. Often the emotional and psychological wounds are even more horrific.

Christine likes to say that A21 takes survivors "from crisis to stability. Human trafficking leaves its mark, but restoration and healing is possible."[8] She knows because she is also a survivor of twelve years of childhood sexual abuse.

Author Max Lucado has said of Christine, "She has the spunk of a Paul. She's scarcely on the stage, or at the dinner table, before you hear her passions: Jesus, her family, and the forgotten girls of the slave trade. You know where she stands. And you know whom she loves. It's contagious, this heart of hers."[9]

Today she works tirelessly to see the healing and wholeness she has found in Christ extended to others. She has written, "I am happily married, with healthy and happy children, living in a loving and safe home, able to come and go and travel the world with purpose and amazing opportunities to teach and to learn myself. My family and I have food, clothing, shelter and health care. My future is filled with dreams, plans, goals, vision. I am free. Yet in the work of A21, and in my travels, I meet so many who are languishing, forgotten, without justice, love, hope, or any promise that their lives—or their children's—may someday get better."[10]

THE HEART OF THE RESCUER

The legacy of rescue. It might be described in the words of the apostle Paul: "So that we may be able to comfort those who are in any affliction, with the comfort with which we ourselves are comforted by God" (2 Cor. 1:4 ESV). As with Jehosheba, it may be that we need to act in the moment. When we see the need, we act with a heart of compassion. Or as with Harriet Tubman, we look into our past and recognize what we've been delivered from. Often it seems that when God delivers us from something, He wants that area of deliverance to become a personal point of ministry. Or perhaps we just need to see better. As with Christine Caine, God might well be asking us to see some things that are not pretty.

Here's the great encouragement. We know that there are many women around this country who are called to rescue, whether because of their background or because of what they are seeing. And as women act on that calling with compassion and courage, we will have a profound impact on our world. Few causes bring us more in line with the heart of our redeeming God, who sent His Son to "proclaim liberty to the captives" (Luke 4:18 NKJV). Each of us has only one life, and what better way to spend it than just as Jesus did—on the lasting work of rescue.

CHAPTER 7

THE LEGACY OF COMPASSION

*Kindness is a language which the deaf can
hear and the blind can see.*

—Anonymous

ome might define faith solely by doctrine and study. We believe, though, that as Francis Schaeffer once said, "there is nothing more ugly than a Christian orthodoxy without understanding or without compassion."[1] Compassion is not only seeing the pain and hurt around you but taking action to help. Of course, compassion was a hallmark of the Messiah's life and ministry. Time and again, the Gospels reveal that Jesus was stirred with compassion for the hurting, the outcast, and the desperate. He was more than sympathetic. He was moved to action. How does compassion inspire *us* to move?

The Life of Compassion Changes History

Ahmose is fighting her daily battle against her archenemy—boredom. She is losing. Again.

As the pampered daughter of the pharaoh, the great ruler of Egypt, she has a life that is easy but monotonous. A team of handmaidens sees to her every whim, and a contingent of palace guards assures her safety and escorts her everywhere she goes. From the time she rises in the morning until she retires at night, she is attended to and watched over. She has everything a young woman could ever desire, except the precious commodity of privacy—and purpose. She longs for something meaningful, significant, and real in her life.

So on this day, she announces her intention to engage in the one permissible activity that can guarantee her a sliver of space and freedom. She will bathe in the Nile—an activity that is more of a spiritual exercise than an act of hygiene.

The Nile is considered sacred by her people, the source of all life, and ritual bathing spots are located near the temples dedicated to Egypt's numerous deities. The site for royal bathing will be discreetly screened by reeds and bulrushes, as well as fenced off beneath the surface of the water to keep hungry crocodiles away. When she bathes in this way, the guards must stand at a distance. Only her chief handmaiden accompanies her to the water's edge. Thus these mornings at the river represent an oasis of privacy in her dreary desert of privilege. Even so, Ahmose approaches the river today with some trepidation.

Several months earlier, her father had decreed that every boy born among the oppressed Hebrew minority of Egypt must be seized and thrown into the Nile. Since then, not a day has gone by that she has not heard the distant wails and shrieks of Hebrew mothers who have had their newborn baby boys torn from their arms and tossed as sacrifices to the crocodiles in the river. On her last walk along the banks, she saw no fewer than a dozen tiny infant bodies floating slowly northward, an image she has been unable to erase from her mind.

As she and her most trusted handmaiden reach the water, she scans the surface, dreading what she might see. After a moment, her eyes fall on something unusual caught among the bulrushes. It appears to be a tar-blackened woven basket of some sort. She dispatches her maidservant to retrieve the strange object.

The little ark is placed gently before her, and Ahmose takes a deep breath before removing the cover of woven reeds. There she beholds the beautiful little face of a baby, swaddled tightly in a blanket bearing a common Hebrew pattern. As the bright sunlight hits his face, his eyes crinkle, his lips pucker, and the most pitiful cry follows. Somehow the forlorn wail seems to carry a healing warmth that melts the heart of the isolated, purposeless princess.

SOMETIMES COMPASSION BREAKS THE RULES

The sensible thing to do is order her servant to fling the crying infant into the river to drown like the thousands of other Hebrew newborns in recent months. Her father would approve of that action. A less extreme but safe approach would be to simply take the basket back to the river and set it afloat once more. Let the strange, invisible God of the Hebrews determine the baby boy's fate.

Ahmose's heart will not let her consider either option. The seed of a sense of purpose begins to germinate in her soul. Her mind races. *Destiny has brought this child to me. I must find a way to preserve his life and raise him as my own. But how?* She must break the rules. She must do what is unconventional and even against what she imagines her father would want her to do.

At that moment, a young Hebrew girl who has been watching in hiding reveals herself and meekly offers a suggestion. She knows a Hebrew woman who has recently given birth and could serve as a wet nurse for the infant until he is weaned. Ahmose does not know that this is the infant's sister, who has been following the basket downstream to monitor his fate. Nor does she know that the proposed wet nurse is the boy's mother.

The princess agrees. However, before she releases her just-adopted infant back to the care of this Hebrew girl, she gives her new son a proper Egyptian name. She calls him Moses, a name rooted in the Egyptian word meaning "to draw out." On this day, she walked down to the river's edge empty and adrift. Yet it was there that she drew forth a sense of purpose from the life-giving waters. Acting with compassion has a way of changing us like that.

Ahmose cannot know it, but a day will come when her Moses will similarly draw his kinsmen out of Egypt. When that baby boy is an old man, having successfully led the twelve tribes of Israel to freedom and into covenant with the God who chose them, he will write of this day. He will relate the details just as he heard them from the lips of the tenderhearted young woman who lived them: "When she opened it, she saw the child, and behold, the baby wept. So she had compassion on him" (Ex. 2:6 NKJV).

ACTING WITH COMPASSION TODAY

My (Lauren's) generation, the millennials, need to be reminded that compassion is showing the love of Christ. In our very divided world, our first act of compassion ought to be seeking first to understand others before being understood. Too often, compassion can be crowded out by busy schedules and overstuffed to-do lists. I'm afraid the busyness of our lives today is more often about our own pursuits, goals, and ambitions, or things that please us individually. As with Ahmose, there's also an uneasy feeling in our world—a boredom with life that leaves too many people caught up with more of their favorite fashion or the latest movie. On the other hand, as with Ahmose, when we live with compassion, our lives change.

For me (Jackie), keeping in mind that the Bible says God's (and mankind's) ancient enemy "prowls around like a roaring lion, seeking someone to devour" (1 Peter 5:8 NASB) is so important. In the wild, a predatory animal looks for the young, the weak, and the wounded. Then the predator will seek to separate the vulnerable one from the herd. Isn't this exactly what Satan does? Isolation is one of our great enemies today.

Do you know someone who is cut off? Someone who sits outside the circle of conversation? I've learned not to let the depressed or hurting person remain isolated. Our human reflex is to just leave them alone until they snap out of it. All their signals may say, "Leave me alone," but that is the worst possible outcome. We have to draw them out like the Egyptian princess drew Moses out of the deadly waters of the Nile.

This also means we should not allow ourselves to become isolated either. We were created for connection and relationship. We need a community of others who can keep us accountable, speak truth into our lives, and hold us up when we're weak. For me, that community is a group of women who call themselves Therapy Group.

After being part of a Bunco group for years (Bunco is a social dice game, usually with twelve players), we decided to disband and use our valuable time to fulfill other needs in our lives. Several years ago, I got together with a group of Christian women, and we made a commitment to gather monthly for fellowship, connection, and prayer. At this point in our lives, we all had different responsibilities and expectations; some now had adult children, while others were still in the midst of parenting young children. Some of our group were now single and working to support themselves. We all had our own struggles to face, as well as our seasons to rejoice, such as weddings and new births. What better way to go through all of those life experiences than with other women who will love us unconditionally, cry with us when we hurt, pray for us in our sorrow, and rejoice with us in our victories? We regularly receive a group text with heartfelt prayer needs. What a privilege it is to walk through life with a group who will go before the Lord on my behalf and whom I can pray for and serve God with. Having a group of believers who are committed to love, serve, and support each other through thick and thin helps keep at bay the lies that come from a spirit of loneliness and isolation.

We're all flawed and far from perfect, yet we know that God has no choice but to use imperfect people. We are His plan A to reach the distressed and hurting.

As we give compassion to others, we've got to receive it for ourselves too. This group has been such a source of strength, encouragement, and godly wisdom for me. We love well. We laugh well. We try to serve one another and others well.

If you don't have people in your life who can fulfill that role, I strongly encourage you to pray about starting to build a group like mine, and I would start that process at a strong, Bible-centered church. You may be surprised at the blessing it will be for you to pray for others. Praying for others helps us think of their needs but also keeps in focus our dependence on God. On the other hand, so many times I've experienced renewed strength when other people have prayed for me. I have been so blessed to have these compassionate women to walk beside me.

When we think about women of the past who built lasting legacies through the power of compassion, many examples come to mind. Few legacies have saved and improved the quality of lives more than the one established by a homeschooled girl from England who defied convention, pressed through resistance, and broke barriers to fulfill God's call on her life.

Discovering a Legacy of Compassion

Everyone wants to discover and live out their calling. Yet calling is typically not discovered because of a lightning bolt or burning bush. More often, calling is discovered as God writes consistent themes on your heart. Our job is to pay attention to those themes.

At the funeral of Florence Nightingale in 1910, a British noble summed up the theme of her remarkable ninety years: "working . . . in a pure spirit of duty towards God and compassion for man."[2] The discovery of her theme, however, began in 1820. Born that year to a wealthy, well-connected family, she had an interesting blend of theological influences as she was growing up. Her parents were raised Unitarian, but as adults they were prominent in the Anglican church. On the other hand, her paternal grandmother was a fiery evangelical, and Florence caught a deep appreciation for the teachings and example of John Wesley. The writings of Jacob Abbott, an American Congregational minister, struck a chord in her heart when she was a teenager, and they crystalized her thinking about the necessity of faith, love, and action working together.

Nightingale credited Abbott's book *The Corner-Stone* with cementing her conversion experience. Abbott's writings also gave her a powerful conviction that God crafted creation to operate in accordance with His natural and spiritual laws. She believed—correctly, we think—that much sickness, disease, and human suffering resulted from either not knowing or disregarding the principles found in God's Word or plainly displayed in His creation. The key to Christian progress on earth involved discovering and applying these principles in compassion-fueled efforts to ease pain.

To Abbott, and to Florence, works of compassion were not to earn or merit God's favor but should flow naturally as a product of having received Christ's forgiveness. In *The Corner-Stone*, Abbott wrote concerning the priest and the Levite in Jesus' parable of the good Samaritan, "They pass by on the other side. Ah, that reveals the secret! A man may devote his life to the external service of God, without really loving him at all; but he can not really love him, and yet pass by and neglect a distressed and suffering brother."[3]

Florence grasped that compassion wasn't a means to

salvation. It was evidence of it. We don't help others in order to attain God's favor; we stand in God's favor because we stand on the cornerstone of Christ's finished work, thereby freeing us from self-centeredness. In the words of Jesus, "Freely you have received; freely give" (Matt. 10:8).

THE CALL OF COMPASSION TAKES SHAPE

A governess taught Florence music and art. Her father oversaw lessons in Greek, Latin, Italian, German, French, English grammar, philosophy, mathematics, and history. Florence also loved books and read voraciously, displaying an insatiable appetite for knowledge as well as a knack for systematizing, categorizing, and organizing.

At the same time, her faith made her uncomfortable living the pampered life of the typical British socialite in the Victorian era. It felt frivolous and frothy to this brilliant girl with a biblical worldview. So even in her teen years, Florence began to seek God's will concerning her life and calling.

On February 7, 1837, just before her seventeenth birthday, she sensed a clear, if unspecific, confirmation from heaven that God had something special in mind for her. She confided to a friend in a letter, "God spoke to me and called me to His Service. What form this service was to take the voice did not say."[4]

What *was* very clear to Nightingale was that much human suffering and unnecessary death could be alleviated or prevented by simply applying what she viewed as God-ordained principles of sanitation, hygiene, and improved organization wherever the sick were cared for. It seemed equally clear to the systems-minded young woman that the most efficient way to accomplish this was to reform the nursing profession. And that, of course, began with becoming a nurse.

Florence's parents were mortified. They emphatically refused to allow their bright, beautiful, cultured daughter to enter an occupation that carried roughly the same status in society as that of a maid. The disappointment plunged the precocious teen into depression for a time. Her parents sought to distract her with a trip to Egypt, but it served only to fan the flames of her burning concern for the poor. While on that trip, she wrote the following prayer of consecration in her journal: "O God, Thou puttest into my heart this great desire to devote myself to the sick and sorrowful. I offer it to Thee. Do with it what is for Thy service."[5]

So Florence clandestinely carried on studies and correspondence exploring the latest scientific understanding of topics like infection, hygiene, sanitation, and epidemic theory. Part of her secret study involved a keen interest in the work of Elizabeth Fry in Germany. Fry, a Quaker, had already made her name as England's leading advocate for prison reform when she launched an experiment in health care at a prison hospital in Kaiserwerth, Germany, in 1840. Florence's father eventually relented somewhat and allowed her to travel to Germany to examine firsthand the work of Fry's deaconesses there.

Everything changed for Nightingale with the outbreak of the Crimean War in 1853. This bloody and protracted conflict pitted Russia against an alliance of France, Britain, and the Ottoman Turks. Soon reports of horrific death rates among Britain's wounded and sick soldiers began to appear in the British newspapers. At the infamous siege of Sevastopol, 2,755 British soldiers died in combat, but another 2,000 died later of their wounds, while more than 16,000 died simply of disease.

As it happened, within months of the war's outbreak, Florence received a letter from Britain's secretary of war, a friend of the Nightingale family, asking Florence to organize a corps of nurses willing to be deployed to staunch the appalling losses of British soldiers to infected wounds and diseases. Florence knew in her heart that this was what she had been preparing for her entire life.

She assembled a team of thirty-eight trained nurses from various religious orders and sailed to the Scutari Barracks in Turkey, an ancient citadel on the Asian side of the straits of Istanbul that had been assigned to the British for use as a hospital. When Florence arrived at the facility, she found horrifying conditions and indescribable human suffering. To their everlasting credit, Florence and her team rolled up their sleeves and waded into the filth and gore, routinely working twenty-four-hour shifts and battling to keep a positive attitude. In a letter to a doctor friend back home, Florence wrote, "In the midst of this appalling horror (we are steeped up to our necks in blood)—there is good . . ."[6]

Florence and her team were eventually able to reduce the death rate dramatically at Scutari, especially after she succeeded in persuading the British government to renovate the hospital to improve sanitation. Nevertheless, Nightingale's greatest contributions would come in later years.

THE CALL TO COMPASSION ELEVATED

After returning to England, Florence wrote *Notes on Nursing*, the first comprehensive textbook for nurse training. At the same time, she established that nation's first school of professional nursing, and by 1865 the first wave of Nightingale-trained nurses began service in hospitals. Her influence almost immediately jumped the Atlantic, as Nightingale's work served as a guide to nurses in the US Civil War. The Union government consulted her personally about how to organize its field hospitals.

Today Florence Nightingale's name is mainly associated with establishing nursing as a true, respected profession. This is a part of her amazing legacy. Prior to Nightingale's accomplishments, nursing was low-status, miserable, poorly compensated work, on par with scrubbing floors and picking vegetables. Hospitals were often unsanitary pits of suffering and death.

In the second half of her life, Nightingale battled serious health challenges. Even though bedridden for years, she continued to do groundbreaking work in the field of hospital organization, and her influence spread around the world. God honored the prayer of that teenage girl who offered herself up to Him in the service of "the sick and the sorrowful." He led her in pathways that saved countless lives as care for the sick worldwide improved, in part because of her pioneering work. That's quite a legacy through simple compassion.

It may be difficult to imagine pursuing a calling like Florence did. But I (Lauren) like to think that she felt it would be difficult too. No doubt, she felt plenty of fear, doubt, and uncertainty as she stepped onto a path that no one had ever walked before. Her journals reveal a woman who is very much like you or me, a woman who simply did all that she knew to do, continued to trust in a big God, and tried to live each day faithful to His calling.

There is a toughness about Florence Nightingale's compassion that we admire. We know genuine love is gritty. Genuine love means being willing to get your hands dirty for the benefit of others. It's our opinion that we live in a day in which many people mistake sentimentality and emotion for love and compassion. Yet real compassion isn't just feeling for the hurting person. Real love means engaging the whole person as they are, while looking past their imperfections and perceiving who God created them to be. The eyes of love see the value that God sees.

Love also means a willingness to climb down into the pit with the person who can't climb out on their own. In our daily lives here in North America, we may not encounter the kinds of needs Florence Nightingale was called to remedy, but our relational spheres and pathways will almost certainly bring us into contact with the depressed, the addicted, the abused, and those suffering from self-inflicted wounds.

In these cases, we have to be wise. Simply feeling sorry for someone's difficult condition may encourage them to stay in the same place. When all we do is express sympathy without compassion in action, we may draw attention to the problem but not solve it. That attention may be all the person was seeking, instead of a real solution. Compassion sometimes means having the hard conversation. Above all, it means taking our eyes off ourselves so we can see the need around us. The remarkable woman we're about to introduce you to did just that.

Opening Your Heart to Compassion

Do you ever think that maybe your world is too small? Sometimes it's necessary to expand it, even if just a little.

Sarah Bowling was a pastor's wife and Bible teacher in Denver, Colorado. In 2009, she decided to expand her world with a mission trip to East Africa. There a chance encounter changed the course of her life and turned her sense of calling upside down.

Half a world away from the comfort of her Colorado home, she found herself in a foreign and desolate place, in one of the poorest parts of one of the poorest nations on earth—Ethiopia. One day, while Sarah was helping lead a large missions team in a remote area of Ethiopia, she learned about twin newborn girls who had been abandoned in a field. These two infants had been left to die, but the orphanage where Sarah and the team were staying decided to break their guidelines and accept them into their facility.

It was a surreal moment for Sarah when she visited these baby girls, holding their frail and uncertain lives in her arms. When she looked into their faces, she saw some of the most beautiful eyes she'd ever beheld. And they were newborn twins! Sarah and her traveling companions set out to learn what was needed to care for these baby girls, since the orphanage wasn't equipped to care for the needs of infants. Sarah came to learn that most orphanages don't accept babies into their care because of the intense requirements demanded for their survival. Because this age group needs so much more in the way of resources and individualized attention, most orphanages are forced to refuse to accept newborns. Nevertheless, the orphanage where Sarah was staying had dismissed their policy to make an exception for these beautiful twins.

With the purpose of her trip suddenly transformed by these events, Sarah was haunted by several thoughts. The first was, *What would have become of these two babies if they hadn't been found?* The only real question was whether it would have been wild animals or dehydration that claimed them first.

Sarah, a mom of three, also couldn't help thinking about the level of desperation and despair a mother must be feeling to take a step like that. These babies' only crime was to be born in a place where the arrival of even one additional child often sends mothers into crisis. For one hopeless mom, the burden of two new mouths at once clearly proved too much to bear.

As Sarah held the baby girls, she wondered, *What must have gone through that mother's mind as she laid them there in the dirt? Did she weep? Did she cover her ears to block out her babies' cries as she walked away? Did she whisper a prayer for their rescue by some compassionate stranger?*

TAKING ACTION ON YOUR COMPASSION

Another, more pressing question arose in her heart. Now that these precious baby girls were in her arms, what would she do? Would she simply hand them back and walk away? Would she too cover her ears to their cries? Try to pretend she hadn't seen them? As she wrestled with the question of why the Lord had brought her to this particular moment, she was reminded of the story of Moses.

His mother too felt compelled to abandon him. She knew that holding on to him meant certain death for him. We can imagine that she held her baby boy close one last time, smelled his hair, kissed his face, set him gently into that basket of reeds, and sent him down the river with a whispered prayer for his rescue.

As Sarah helped care for those beautiful newborns in the days that followed, God spoke to her clearly. He said, "Sarah, you have a heart for children; I put this in you. I want you to 'save Moses.' I want you to help rescue and care for the smallest, weakest, and most vulnerable who are suffering in the world today."

Through this experience, a new initiative called Saving Moses was born. It's a humanitarian outreach focused on providing vital care for children five and under in the places where it is most urgently needed yet least available.

As Sarah discovered when she began to research the need, the awful truth is that every day twenty-six thousand children under the age of five die.[7] Every single day. The age of five is significant because the deaths of babies and toddlers under five in low-income countries are primarily attributed to causes that are utterly preventable. Yet for reasons we've already examined, many government and humanitarian organizations do not work with infants and toddlers. Still, if a child can reach the age of five, his or her chances of living a full, productive life soar.

Sarah came to Ethiopia with an open heart and left with a new mission: to do what she could to save a generation of Moses-babies. She began by raising funds to provide formula for under-resourced malnutrition clinics in Angola, a nation with one of the highest infant mortality rates on the planet. In the years that followed, the work in Angola broadened and was augmented by programs training midwives in war-torn Afghanistan and other key points of need.

SAYING YES TO MORE

Then in 2012, Sarah's work took another unexpected turn, one that would widen further the already broad borders of Sarah's radical compassion.

On a fact-finding trip to Phnom Penh, Cambodia, Sarah was given a late-night drive through that city's notorious red-light district. As they drove past a seemingly endless string of bars and clubs operating as fronts for brothels, she was shocked to see many infants and toddlers sitting on blankets on the sidewalk. A little investigation revealed that these babies belonged to the prostitutes working in these establishments.

Additional inquiry revealed that these infants were routinely abducted and sold into the same sexual slavery machinery holding their mothers in bondage. Sarah learned that the fear of this ever-present threat leads many mothers to leave their infants and toddlers locked up alone and unattended all night long. Otherwise these little ones end up being forced to work in the sex industry, are viciously abused by their mothers' clients, or are simply left lying next to their mothers while they "work."

She learned of the horrifying generational nature of sexual slavery in this and many other parts of the world, how many of the prostitutes are literally born into the brothels to mothers who themselves were born there.

She learned that Cambodia has one of the largest populations of sex workers in the world. She also discovered that although there are many admirable and important organizations seeking to end the scourge of the sex trade, there was virtually nothing being done to address the heartbreaking daily plight of these innocent infants and toddlers.

In the glaring light of all these revelations, Sarah heard a challenge similar to the one she'd sensed three years earlier in that Ethiopian village—a challenge to go to "the least of these" and present a tangible manifestation of God's love and care for them. Sarah has written, "You don't get much 'least-er' than being a baby born to a prostitute in one of the poorest nations on earth."[8]

In response, Saving Moses opened the first of several Night

Care centers providing safe, nurturing, loving care for infants and toddlers in the overnight hours. The little ones left in their care get a bath, clean clothes, a nutritious meal, time for play, and a lesson and then are put to bed until their mothers pick them up in the morning. The mothers of these babies frequently weep with gratitude to learn that such a safe, loving place exists, and at no cost to them.

Today Saving Moses operates five Night Care centers in Phnom Penh and is planning additional centers in places such as Dhaka, Bangladesh, and Calcutta, India—cities in which huge numbers of women are ensnared in the generational abyss of sex work. It is a cycle of suffering and poverty that Saving Moses has found a compassion-inspired way to break. Sarah says, "We aim to break the cycle of sex work by providing safe, loving care, and ultimately a way out, to the infants and little children of women trapped in the slavery of the sex industry there."

They have discovered firsthand that the best way to reach a mother's heart is to help her protect her most valued treasure, her children. Saving Moses remains focused on its mission to save babies and toddlers. Yet in doing so, they naturally win the trust and capture the hearts of many mothers. Through the caregivers there, the mothers learn of the existence of a world outside the red-light districts and brothels, a world they scarcely knew existed. Whenever a woman expresses interest in finding a pathway to a different life, the organization refers them to trusted groups equipped and called to meet that need.

From Angola to Cambodia, and in many other critical points of need around the world, Sarah and Saving Moses are actively, effectively making a difference in the lives of the most helpless and most vulnerable. And what of those twin newborns who launched Sarah on this journey? As of this writing, they are thriving eight-year-olds, surrounded by love and care.

We should mention that Sarah is the daughter of Bible

teacher Marilyn Hickey, highlighted in chapter 3, so she grew up seeing firsthand what a woman of God can accomplish with courage, commitment to God's Word, and consecration to God's plan. What a wonderful example of legacy.

We recognize that it would be easy to read the stories of Ahmose, Florence Nightingale, and Sarah Bowling and say, "That's not me." That's understandable, because often the thing that holds us back is the comparison trap. Instead our aim and our hope is that you'll look at these stories and see commonality—the threads that bind us all together. Ahmose needed purpose, and she broke some rules to act with compassion. Florence Nightingale followed a lifelong theme of compassion in action. Sarah Bowling was merely a woman looking to broaden her view of the world. And in the end, when they each saw a need, they acted on the need and took simple steps of obedience.

Ahmose, Florence, and Sarah all experienced the same doubts and fears along the way. They are no different than us. They just took the next step God put in front of them, leaving the results up to Him.

And the same invitation is open to you. Will you take the next step God has put in your path? Faithfulness isn't reserved for people who are ready for brave, high-level stunts or dramatic, life-changing decisions. Faithfulness is for all of us when we simply say yes to God and do the next right thing. Sometimes this may be dramatic, but most of the time it will take the shape of obedience in the ordinary.

By now, though, we know that in God's hands all those ordinary acts of obedience add up to a significant legacy.

CHAPTER 8

THE LEGACY OF BOLDNESS

Life is either a daring adventure or nothing.
Avoiding danger is no safer in the long run
than outright exposure. The fearful are
caught as often as the bold.

—Helen Keller[1]

Boldness. Some of us want it. Some of us run from it. It does seem that bold people attract the attention—and the criticism. However, boldness is not something we are just born with. It is and can be cultivated, if we feel we have something worth speaking up for.

Boldness Born of Need

Little does she know the conversation she'll have today. Little does she know the conversation she needs. In the Bible, she's known simply as the Samaritan woman. Here we give her a name—Avara—to bring the story to life.

With both hands, Avara hoists the long staff and then lowers it onto her shoulders. At each end, dangling from a rope handle, is a large, empty water pot. This is no light burden, but she knows it will be far heavier on the return trip from the well at the edge of her village.

The sun too presses down on her. It is high in the sky and

oppressively hot. Here in the desert of Samaria, the well will be deserted at this hour, and that is precisely the point. The other women of the village headed there at sunrise, while it was still relatively cool, to draw their water for the day. They walked there as a group, both for safety and for socializing. Avara is not welcome in this informal club. She'll see enough stares and glares and hear enough whispers and snickers during her lonely walk through town. She has no appetite for an extra portion of rejection.

Avara is *that* woman. The one who at the age of thirty-two has collected more husbands than most of the village women have children. The first one—from a match arranged by her uncle when she was only fourteen—was forty years her senior. He died in their first year of marriage, leaving her destitute. Several subsequent husbands were either abusive or drunkards or both. A few years ago, homeless, alone, and out of options, she accepted an invitation to live with a man on the far edge of town who had recently been released from a Roman jail. With her reputation in the community already in tatters, she didn't even bother to get married.

Fiery, feisty, and intelligent, Avara pretends not to care what the other women think. Underneath the facade and bravado, however, there's a rumbling need, a restlessness that she can't put a finger on.

THE CONVERSATION SHE SHOULDN'T HAVE

While still some distance from the well, Avara is surprised to see the figure of a man sitting under the meager shade of a scrawny tree. Drawing closer brings an even bigger revelation. His manner of dress suggests He is a Jew. This is a sight rarely if ever seen in Samaria.

It is neither safe nor proper for a woman to be alone with a strange man, but Avara presses forward, unafraid. She knows how to take care of herself, and she laughs silently at the fleeting thought of avoiding the appearance of impropriety. That ship sailed long ago. Her entire life has become a display of impropriety. Besides, this religious Jew will certainly withdraw as soon as He sees that she is determined to approach the watering hole. She knows well that for a man of His culture and faith, to speak to a lone woman is forbidden; proximity to a Samaritan woman would be doubly defiling. The Jews view her kind as unclean, and most will walk many miles out of their way to avoid even passing through the territory of people they detest.

She intends to draw her water in silence and leave as quickly as possible, but to her shock, the stranger engages her in conversation. He asks for a drink of water. Finding herself talking to a real, live Jew for the first time in her life, she feels a surge of nationalistic pride. He wants water, but instead she offers Him a debate.

CROSSING THE LINE

Avara tries to bait the stranger with an assertion about the location of the true mountain of God. Her brazen audacity is unheard of in this place and time. She is not only a woman challenging a man; she is a Samaritan woman challenging a Jewish man.

So she braces herself for a response of sputtering, furious indignation. It never comes. Instead, with gentle confidence, He speaks of a coming day in which people everywhere will worship God wherever they happen to be. He says that God desires a new kind of worshiper—one who will worship Him in the Spirit and in truth.

He speaks to her of living water, and He does so in a way that betrays not a shred of condemnation or criticism, even when He begins to reveal a thorough knowledge of the painful details of her life. Those eyes. She'd forgotten what it felt like to be seen as a person rather than as an object—either of desire or revulsion.

In a moment, the granite-hard protective shell around her

heart crumbles. The healing waters of acceptance and unconditional love rush in to quench her parched spirit.

A ray of revelation illuminates the darkness, and suddenly she knows who this extraordinary stranger truly is. Abandoning her water pots, she runs back into the village and finds the leading men of the town in their usual spot in the shade. They are stunned to see this shunned woman run up to them, blurting out the account of her encounter at the well. She suspects He is the promised Messiah. Before she is finished, they will be more than half convinced themselves.

On this day, Avara becomes one of the very first evangelists of the messianic era. Her name stems from the Aramaic root word for blindness or darkness, but historians of the Eastern Church will record that she will soon earn a new name. As the gospel spreads north and west from Jerusalem, she will be known as Photine, a name that in Greek means "illuminated one." Eastern tradition suggests she became an evangelist and died a martyr for proclaiming the message of that stranger at the well. Her legacy is built on boldness—crossing the line by having a conversation that society would say she shouldn't have had and sharing with people who did not accept her.

THE LESSONS OF BOLDNESS

Boldness is a powerful attribute. Yet many assume it is something one is born with. *Either you have it or you don't*, we tend to think. The witness of Scripture, though, is that boldness is often an imparted gift from God that can be sought through prayer. In Psalm 138:3, David declares, "In the day when I cried out, You answered me, and made me bold with strength in my soul" (NKJV). In other passages, it is portrayed as a choice: "Be strong, be bold, don't be afraid or frightened of them, for ADONAI your God is going with you. He will neither fail you nor abandon you" (Deut. 31:6 CJB).

Yet in other places, the Bible portrays confidence and boldness as natural outgrowths of knowing you're in right standing with God: "The wicked run away when no one is chasing them, but the godly are as bold as lions" (Prov. 28:1 NLT).

God used the boldness of the Samaritan woman at the well to start a revival not only in her own heart but also in her village. As believers, we are called to be bold and unapologetic in our witness to a fallen, broken world. In the cause of reaching the unreached, our audacity is fueled by love, for God and for others.

There are other occasions, however, when boldness is required to right a wrong. To correct an ongoing injustice. To fight an ongoing evil. This brand of boldness brings to mind one particular woman of legacy.

The Boldness of Justice

When Rosa Parks was faced with a grave injustice, her faith made her as bold as a lion, and God used her to change the course of American history.

Few Americans are unaware of this woman's remarkable place in history. Most know at least the broad outlines of how, on December 1, 1955, in Montgomery, Alabama, Parks refused to obey a bus driver's order to give up her seat to a white passenger as required by city ordinances. Many know that her arrest kicked off the Montgomery Bus Boycott, which proved to be a turning point in the quest for civil rights and equality.

THE SEEDS OF BOLDNESS

What few realize is that Rosa Parks's boldness was not her natural tendency. Parks considered herself a meek and timid person. She was a shy, quiet child who began memorizing Bible verses while very young. She excelled in reciting Scriptures in Sunday school at the local African Methodist Episcopal (AME) church in tiny Pine Level, Alabama. She once told a biographer, "God is everything to me."[2]

This bent toward spiritual things emerged early and powerfully. As a child, Rosa attended church as often as she could, performed daily devotions, and prayed constantly. It appears that all of this piety emerged organically from Rosa rather than from outward pressure from her mother or grandparents: "I was never pressed, against my will, to go to church. I always wanted to go."[3]

The roots of Rosa's AME denomination are inextricably intertwined with the earliest resistance to slavery among African Americans. The church group was born in Philadelphia in 1816 through the efforts of Bishop Richard Allen, a former slave. From its founding, the AME Church used publications and other writings to encourage the end of slavery at the state level. Prominent early members included abolitionist icons Frederick Douglass, Harriet Tubman, and Sojourner Truth.

Rosa's father left the family when she was very young and reentered her life only sporadically after that. Her mother traveled frequently for short-term teaching opportunities in order to support her young family. Thus Rosa's grandparents became key influences in her life. Her grandfather modeled a quiet but strong defiance in the face of injustice that would emerge in Rosa as an adult, propelling her into the national spotlight in the fight for equality.

Rosa's childhood coincided with a nationwide resurgence of the KKK. It is estimated that in the sixteen-month period between June 1920 and October 1921, eighty-five thousand men joined the Klan across the United States. The majority of these were in northern states such as New Jersey and Indiana. Nevertheless, the rise of Klan 2.0, so to speak, in Alabama resulted in a particularly violent and menacing brand of militant racism.

Poignantly, some of Rosa Parks's earliest childhood memories were of her grandfather keeping a double-barreled shotgun close at hand at all times, loaded and ready to defend his home should any hooded goons burst through the door, looking to harm his family. Rosa remembered, "We talked about how just in case the Klansmen broke into our house, we should go to bed with our clothes on so we would be ready to run if we had to."[4] There were kind white folks in her life, but Rosa realized even at the early age of six that the people in her community "were not actually free."[5]

THE SEEDS OF BOLDNESS BLOSSOM

The quiet, bookish Christian girl grew up, married, and moved to Montgomery—a huge city in the eyes of the girl who had grown up outside the rural, unincorporated township of Pine Level. Throughout her years there, she increasingly chafed at the inherent unfairness and dehumanizing aspects of Montgomery's codified Jim Crow laws.

She tried on three occasions over the span of several years simply to register to vote. She succeeded only on the third try. Particularly onerous to Rosa—perhaps in part because it was an unavoidable element of her daily routine—were Montgomery's laws governing segregated bus seating.

Black passengers dependent on Montgomery's buses were subjected to complex and unevenly applied rules, all of which were humiliating. Enforcement varied from driver to driver, each of whom was endowed with police powers.

Each city bus had a front door and another near the rear. Montgomery's rules required black passengers to enter at the front door to pay, and then get back off the bus and reenter through the rear. Apparently, some drivers thought it a humorous prank to pull away before the passenger, who had already paid his or her fare, could make it through the rear door.

The front ten seats on each bus were reserved for whites,

even if no white passengers were on the bus. The ten rearmost seats were for black passengers. The middle seats were to be assigned by the driver, depending on the racial composition of the passenger load. The laws explicitly stated that if instructed to do so by the driver, a black passenger in any seat, regardless of location on the bus, must surrender his or her seat to a white passenger. This was the law that Rosa Parks would violate in 1955 in an act of principled civil disobedience. The driver's name in that event was James F. Blake.

In 1943, twelve years before her history-making act of defiance, Rosa experienced a prelude. On that day, she boarded a bus driven by the same James Blake. As it happened, the entire back half of the bus was filled with black passengers, both seated and standing. Even the stairway of the rear entrance was full of standing passengers.

Rosa entered the bus in the front, paid her fare, and because of the congestion at the rear entrance, continued down the aisle to the rear half of the bus to stand, even though there were empty seats in the front half of the bus. When she turned around, the driver was staring at her angrily. He ordered her to get off the bus and go to the back door to get on. She refused. She was already in the back and saw no need to get off only to get back on again. Blake began yelling at her, saying that if she did not get off and get back on through the back door, she would need to get off "his bus." When she refused to move, Blake grabbed her coat sleeve and pulled her forward. She did not resist, but near the front of the bus, a flustered Rosa dropped her purse. As she would later describe the incident, "Rather than stoop or bend over to get it, I sat right down in the front seat and from a sitting position I picked up my purse."[6]

This simple act of sitting momentarily in a front seat was deeply symbolic, and that symbolism wasn't lost on anyone who witnessed it. For a moment Rosa thought Blake might strike her, but he did not. She exited the bus and walked away, furious, embarrassed, and shaken. From that day forward, she routinely checked who was driving a bus before boarding it.

As we know, Mrs. Parks would encounter this driver again twelve years later. She had not planned her act of defiance on that December day in 1955. She could not have. She had no way of knowing that her old nemesis would demand that she surrender her seat to a white man.

Yet when that demand came, something arose inside her. A long-time-in-coming no swelled up within her spirit, and in that moment a meek, shy, Jesus-loving woman became very bold. She was arrested, booked, and jailed.

That boldness initially stunned and then galvanized a fragmented black community in Montgomery. Many local pastors of black churches who up to that point had largely stood on the sidelines in the battle against segregation in Montgomery suddenly entered the fray. One of these was the twenty-five-year-old pastor of the Dexter Avenue Baptist Church. His name: Martin Luther King Jr.

Rosa's no led to the Montgomery Bus Boycott, which grabbed national headlines and set in motion the sequence of events that led to the dismantling of immoral segregationist laws all over the nation.

Of course, Rosa Parks's act of defiance involved an enormous personal risk. That is the nature of creating a legacy through boldness. Yet risk taking, the willingness to make mistakes, the willingness to look foolish in front of others, to be criticized and misunderstood, is the very thing so many of us find difficult.

We can all take heart in the boldness of Rosa Parks. Boldness does not belong only to those of great intelligence or stature. Instead boldness belongs to people who, like Rosa, cultivate a gentle spirit of faith but finally grow weary of the injustice around them. Sometimes instead of accepting unfairness as "just the way it is," we need to put aside our fears and insufficiencies, using wisdom and the Holy Spirit as our guide, and speak boldly.

These fears and concerns are universal but seem to be especially present for younger women. Which makes it all the more encouraging that one of the boldest, clearest voices championing biblical truth and faith in our post-Christian era is an Oxford-educated scholar who is also a wife and mother.

Will You Boldly Defend Your Faith?

In a field traditionally populated by men, *Christianity Today* magazine called Amy Orr-Ewing "Oxford's Unapologetic Female Apologist."[7] As you may know, Christian apologetics is the vital but challenging field concerned with defending the Christian faith against skeptics and doubters. Our English word *apology* springs from a Greek word that means "to give a defense." Christian apologetics, then, is the art and science of giving a defense of the Christian faith.

Let's step back for a moment. We live in a culture in which attacks on the Christian faith are a regular occurrence. Sometimes that criticism is warranted. And sometimes it is not. In either circumstance, how do you respond? Do you feel equipped to present a reasoned defense of your beliefs? Do you boldly speak up and point out the fallacies or falsehoods being proclaimed? Many of us remain silent and passive in such situations. Most of us don't feel equipped to defend what we believe. We've never needed bold defenders of the faith more urgently.

Throughout the history of the church, God has raised up skilled champions to defend biblical faith on reasoned, intellectual terms, refuting critics from the fields of science and philosophy on their own terms. Paul and John were two of the very first defenders of the faith. Our New Testament contains treasured passages in which these apostles addressed the most common objections to the gospel message at the time of their writing and refuted the most dangerous heretical attacks on the faith in the earliest days of the infant church.

Notable Christian apologists through the centuries have included Augustine, Thomas Aquinas, and Blaise Pascal. In the mid-twentieth century, C. S. Lewis and Francis Schaeffer stepped forward to present a compelling defense of the faith against modern skeptics. More recently, Norman Geisler, Josh McDowell, Lee Strobel, and Ravi Zacharias have risen to that same challenge.

It is under the mentorship of Zacharias that Amy Orr-Ewing has emerged to become a leader who has "faced the toughest audiences on the global scene, and when she is finished with her presentations, even the strident skeptic responds with respect for the integrity of her defense."[8] Amy also recently has been voted one of the UK's one hundred most influential Christians. In a post-Christian culture, she has chosen to devote her "only one life" to defending the lasting truths of Christ.

THROUGH HUMILIATION AN APOLOGIST ARISES

How did this remarkable woman find the path to becoming the person Alister McGrath, Oxford University's professor of historical theology, called "one of the finest young Christian communicators of our day"?[9] How did she get so bold?

According to Amy, the answer lies in an embarrassing incident among some peers when she was just a preteen girl. She recalls being asked point-blank by another girl if she believed in the Bible. Suddenly she found herself fumbling to construct shallow arguments from fragments she vaguely remembered from C. S. Lewis and Francis Schaeffer. Her hastily constructed defense didn't work. She was met with wave after wave of laughter and teasing by her peers.

Amy never forgot the feeling of helplessness and frustration at not being able to give a more coherent, persuasive argument for her beliefs. That frustration launched her toward a calling not only to engage and refute the intellectual, academic critics of biblical Christianity but also to help equip her fellow believers to make a strong case for their faith outside the walls of academia or the church.

Today Amy exemplifies boldness as director of the Oxford Centre for Christian Apologetics (OCCA), and as Europe, the Middle East, and Africa director for Ravi Zacharias International Ministries (RZIM). This lovely blonde mother of three boys with a winning smile is a world-class academic. She earned a degree with highest honors in theology at Oxford's Christ Church before moving on to a master's in theology at King's College, London. She has also just been awarded a PhD from Oxford University.

MY MILLENNIAL REFLECTIONS ON BOLDNESS

As a member of the millennial generation myself, I (Lauren) am encouraged that Amy and her husband have focused on equipping the church to reach skeptical millennials raised in a thoroughly postmodern culture. Their 2010 book *Millennials: Reaching and Releasing the Rising Generation*[10] is a wonderful source for churches and ministries looking for guidance on making the gospel accessible to my generation.

Of course, the fact that Amy has just completed a doctoral degree while I am working on mine causes me to identify with and admire her even more, especially because she did so as the mother of three boys while maintaining a demanding speaking schedule. When my PhD program seems stressful or overwhelming as I'm working full-time and having speaking opportunities as well, Amy's life encourages me that I'm not the only one!

Amy's calling requires boldness. But she didn't choose this path because she is naturally bold. Rather she has found boldness arising within her because she has obediently and faithfully followed God's call onto this path. That has certainly been my experience.

I am an introvert by nature who, growing up, never ever wanted to be the focus of attention. I was the kid who dreaded giving oral reports and wouldn't even ask a question in class for fear of speaking in front of others. My parents like to tell the story of how, when I turned sixteen and applied for a job at one of our Hobby Lobby stores, I pleaded not to be assigned to work at a cash register, where I would have to interact with strangers. To my great relief, my pleas were heard, and I was given a job working in the seasonal department, stocking shelves and unpacking merchandise deliveries. I was *that* shy.

Nevertheless, throughout my twenties, things changed. As Hobby Lobby grew in the public eye, more and more speaking opportunities presented themselves, not all of which could be handled by Mom, Dad, or other members of the family. One day, my dad asked me if I would want to go speak at an event in his place. I knew it was an opportunity to share stories of God's work, so I accepted. In the days leading up to that first speech, I was so nervous! I slept only a few hours the night before. After giving the speech, I felt like I had done terribly. And that venue never asked me to speak again, so maybe they thought so too! But as I practiced more and had more opportunity, I began to grow in my ability. The girl who didn't want to work at the cash register was now in front of groups, sometimes large groups, speaking. God has a sense of humor! Needless to say, I was consistently pulled out of my comfort zone. I also found that the process caused me to rely more fully on God. And whenever I did, a boldness I didn't know I possessed arose and carried me through.

THE ADVENTURE OF BOLDNESS

Amy combines a gift for persuasive, Bible-based reasoning with a heart to give people in restricted nations an opportunity to read that miraculous book for themselves. She and her husband, Francis, known to all as "Frog," have engaged in several clandestine mission trips, smuggling Bibles into areas closed to Christian worship and witness.

Amy and Frog were only dating and barely nineteen years of age in 1996 when they opted to spend their spring break posing as young journalism students on a fact-finding trip to Afghanistan. In reality, they were carrying desperately needed Pashto translations of the Bible. At that very time, the Taliban was in the final stages of consolidating their brutal grip on that nation and imposing the most extreme expression of Islamic Sharia law the world had ever seen. It seems boldness has been a part of Amy's makeup for quite some time.

In the two decades since then, Amy has become one of the most effective and sought-after speakers on college campuses in the UK, as well as across Europe and in America and Australia. Of course, she occasionally speaks in churches and Christian conferences, but rather than preach to the choir, she much prefers to go where the skeptics and doubters are and to engage them with well-reasoned arguments in her winsome way. She says, "The whole purpose is to engage with people who don't agree with you already."[11]

That's why she and other team members from the Oxford Centre for Christian Apologetics routinely hold events on university campuses, including free lunchtime question-and-answer sessions and evening lectures. Hundreds of students come to Christ each year through these and similar OCCA events. A favorite topic for Amy in these settings is the question, "Can we trust the Bible?"

In this presentation, Amy takes her listeners through the origins of Scripture, pointing out that even though the New Testament was compiled from more than five thousand manuscripts, it tells a very unified and consistent story. She then presents various lines of evidence for the historic authenticity of the Gospels. Some of the most striking of these are also the simplest. She points to research that reveals the most popular male names in first-century Palestine, and points out how these names appear repeatedly in the Gospels. If the Gospels were forged at a later date, they would not be filled with names specific to that time period. This minor piece of evidence is just one example of many proving the accuracy of the Gospels. Places, geography, culture, architecture, and botany—all testify to the reality that the Bible ought to be taken seriously.

OUR PERSONAL ENCOURAGEMENT TO BOLDNESS

Like Lauren, I (Jackie) have found myself stretched far beyond my comfort zone—the domestic roles I had taken on. Our family has made a substantial commitment of time, effort, and resources toward the creation of the new Museum of the Bible in Washington, D.C. We, along with our family, have been the lead donor, and my husband, Steve, chairs the board. Because of my efforts to help with the museum in many ways since its inception, some have called me "the first lady of the museum." But more deeply, bringing the Bible to the world by way of the museum has become the central message and calling in my life.

When the Museum of the Bible project sprang to life in 2009, I was fully engaged in being a wife, mother, and grandmother. It was a pretty normal life, consisting of getting the kids to school, driving them to and from school activities and lessons, helping them with homework in the evenings, and sometimes babysitting grandchildren. I served on a private school board and a crisis pregnancy center board, was involved in my local church, and occasionally joined my husband on business trips. But as Steve became more deeply involved in the museum efforts, the doors opened for me to become more involved too.

When we realized that we weren't just donating artifacts to

a museum that others would create but would be spearheading the efforts ourselves, we felt God calling us to give it our all. With our two youngest children still at home, we had a serious discussion with them and shared what we felt God was calling us to do. I told them that I believed that if He was calling their dad and me, then I wondered if they felt Him calling them too, since they would be greatly impacted by our mission. They said they were in agreement, but each child had a question.

Our youngest, who was five years old at the time, asked, "Will I have to go on stage?"

That was the last thing I expected her to say. I said, "Well, do you *want* to go on the stage?"

She replied, "No! But you can take all of the money I have saved in my piggy bank and give it to the museum." Her generous spirit warmed my heart.

Then my eleven-year-old piped up with her question. "Could we negotiate something?"

Oh boy. I wondered where this was going. "Absolutely! What is it?"

"Could we make a commitment as a family to have one night of real quality time together at least once a month?" That's my 'quality time' girl! I was so proud of all my children and how supportive they were as we embarked on a journey that took more time, effort, and prayer than we ever imagined. We were all in agreement and felt called and committed.

Of course, what I couldn't anticipate was that soon I'd be asked to join Steve on the stage as a speaker. That was something I had never dreamed I would be doing. And to be honest, I wasn't even sure I could do what was being asked of me. I found myself standing before hundreds of people at a time!

Over and over, I've felt inadequate, unqualified, unprepared. And each time, I've had to practice what I've always proclaimed: go to God and His Word in humble recognition that I can't do this in my own strength, but in assurance that I will find a supply of whatever I need to carry out God's will. This is certainly true of boldness, but it's also true of all the attributes we're highlighting on these pages. Are you facing circumstances that will require more wisdom than you think you possess? Go to the Word. Feeling inadequate in the areas of compassion, tenacity, or courage? The reserves and resources you need are there as you prayerfully put Scripture into your mind and heart.

I know this to be true, because this is my testimony. God is faithful to show up and work within my insufficiencies. So it is no surprise that Lauren and I are cheering on women like Amy Orr-Ewing who are championing the Bible in our dark, skeptical world.

A FINAL WORD ON BOLDNESS

I (Lauren) am especially encouraged to see how the OCCA recognizes the power of Christian women to use their inherent strengths, such as relationship skills and emotional intelligence, to persuade and advocate for the cause of Christ. Today ten of RZIM's forty-two traveling apologists in the region comprising Europe, Middle East, and Africa are women.

Amy inspires and challenges me to be bolder as I pursue my own PhD in a program in which I am the first-ever female student.

As I write this, I'm in classes in which there will be me and a bunch of men sitting at a round table debating and discussing ideas and theology. I periodically have to lead our discussion on our assigned reading. If you had told me several years ago that I would be doing that, I would have suggested that you'd lost your mind. Facilitating discussions with a group of men would not have been on my to-do list! Yet as I follow the path of my deepest convictions, I'm finding boldness and courage I never knew I possessed. I'm okay with being the lone woman in the room. I feel honored to be a voice for the things I care deeply about.

We live in a complex time. Never has there been a time when so many lines have been drawn in the sand in our culture wars. It is a tense and contentious time. Speaking up about faith and convictions can be hard, especially when there are real consequences for not holding the views that our culture praises. I so appreciate the thoughtful Christian voices, like Amy Orr-Ewing, who are speaking with kindness and conviction, and doing so in a winsome way, without backing down from their beliefs. Hearing their thoughtful defenses of the faith has inspired me to rise to the same level. I want to learn to think well about the difficult, complex, and often divisive issues that relate to faith and the public square.

But boldness doesn't require a PhD. It can simply mean being honest about our beliefs concerning the issues of the day when we're out to lunch with our friends. It can mean living with integrity in the workplace or saying something when we hear prejudice enter a conversation. Wherever we are, we can speak up about what's right and what we believe.

We are living in a day in which Christian women need boldness more than ever. Just a few decades ago, our society still shared general agreement about matters of faith, family, and freedom. Unfortunately, it seems we've reached a point where our society now pressures us to downplay our Christian faith. This suppression of faith begs for boldness. The apostle Paul also lived in a day in which he was called to present the truth of the gospel to a godless culture. Acts 28:31 says, "He proclaimed the kingdom of God and taught about the Lord Jesus Christ—with all boldness and without hindrance!" May the same be said of us in our time.

CHAPTER 9

THE LEGACY OF TENACITY

*I have one desire now—to live a life of
reckless abandon for the Lord, putting all my
energy and strength into it.*

—Elisabeth Elliot[1]

Tenacious—we love that word. It means persistent.
Determined. Even stubborn (in a good way). How many
great things happen simply because we hang in there? How
many things do we miss out on because we give up too soon?

The Power of a Persistent Mother

News of a wonder-working rabbi in Galilee has spread north
into the borderlands of Tyre and Sidon, Gentile districts that in
the distant future will be within the borders of a place called
Lebanon. Traveling merchants carry stories of a Jewish preacher
who draws crowds of astonishing size, opens blind eyes, heals
all forms of diseases, and even raises the dead.

Some locals dismiss these reports as fables concocted by
their excitable Jewish neighbors to the south. Donatiya does
not. She believes.

Something in her heart has always sensed that the unseen
God of the Jewish people was unlike the idols of her Canaanite
ancestors or the myriad of deities worshiped by the Romans in

their ubiquitous marble temples. So the rumors of the Galilean rabbi's miracles always stirred her soul.

Now rumors are circulating that this holy man is nearby! Supposedly, He and a small group of His disciples are traveling on the road between two nearby villages. Donatiya feels a surge of hope. Her precious little daughter has been cruelly tormented for years by a demonic spirit. If there is anyone who can set her daughter free, it must be this Jesus. So Donatiya arranges for a relative to care for her daughter and heads across open pastures to intercept the travelers. She does not know what she will say to Jesus, but she knows that she must see Him. As she hurries through fields dotted with sheep and goats, there are several things she cannot possibly know.

She does not know that Jesus has slipped away from Galilee and into this Gentile region because He needs to get away from the constant, pressing demands of the crowds. He is exhausted. Nor could she possibly comprehend the full nature of His life and mission. His mission is not merely to heal a few people in one small corner of the world; it is much bigger. He's come to reverse the curse of a sin-stained world for all time and make eternal life available to whoever would come to Him and believe. He has come to restore all that was lost in the fall of mankind—to disarm the principalities of darkness that torment her child.

She cannot understand the nature of His mission. His first priority is to preach the gospel of God's kingdom to His Jewish brothers and sisters. All Donatiya knows is that her beloved daughter is a prisoner and this Jesus might hold the key to her freedom.

She presses forward until she gets to the road on which the men were reported to be traveling. She strains to see where the road meets the horizon, and spots what appears to be about a dozen figures moving away from her. She gathers her skirts and runs as fast as her legs will carry her.

Reaching the men, she follows at a respectful distance until she catches her breath. It does not surprise her when they pretend not to notice her. She knows that the most religious of the Jews don't interact with Gentiles. Finally, she musters the courage to call to Him.

Maintaining her distance, she shouts, "Have mercy on me, O Lord, Son of David! For my daughter is possessed by a demon that torments her severely." A couple of the rabbi's followers turn to glare in her direction while the group as a whole continues walking. It's awkward. It's uncomfortable. She shouts her plea again. And again there is no response.

The silence from the group sends an unmistakable message. She is not wanted. She should leave. But she is determined. The hope in Donatiya burns too hot to be quenched so easily. She cries out again and again. She follows at the same strategic distance—not too close, yet just close enough.

Eventually, she hears some of the exasperated disciples turn to their leader and implore Him to send her away. Her heart leaps into her throat as He turns and approaches her. She searches His face for any sign of His intentions. She sees weary determination, yet there is kindness in His eyes. Now a small crowd of locals from the village ahead begins to gather. He speaks.

"Dear lady, my assignment is God's lost sheep—the people of Israel."

In response, Donatiya falls to her knees in a posture of worship. Having looked into His eyes, she is even more convinced that He is the answer to her pain and that she must find a way to persuade Him.

"Lord, help me."

The Nazarene studies her for a moment and then says, in a voice just loud enough for the bystanders to hear, "It's not right to take food meant for the children of the house and throw it to puppies." A number of people gasp and murmur angrily at His obvious meaning. Offended on her behalf, they exhort her to leave. She doesn't.

So matter-of-fact is Jesus' pronouncement that Donatiya fully expects Him to turn and walk away. Yet He doesn't. He just stands there looking at her, clearly waiting for her response—a response the crowd doesn't want her to give. Suddenly she hears a rebuttal, a cry for mercy, coming out of her mouth.

"True enough, sir, but even puppies under the table get the crumbs that fall to the ground!"

She holds her breath, awaiting whatever is going to happen next. After a second or two, she sees one eyebrow arch. A twinkle flashes in His eyes, and the hint of a smile creeps across His face. After an eternity of a few more seconds, she hears these words:

"Dear woman, your faith is great. Your request is granted."

She knows instantly it is true. Tears begin to flow in a river of joy and relief. Donatiya chokes out her thanks between sobs and withdraws. Arriving at home, she sees with her own eyes what her heart has already acknowledged. Her daughter is free.

THE LESSONS OF PERSISTENCE

Throughout the history of the church, the example of the nameless Syrophoenician, whom we have dubbed Donatiya, has inspired generations of intercessors to persist in prayer even when the desired answer from heaven did not come immediately. We have given her a name here to help us see this familiar episode in a new way—through her eyes.

However, this desperate Gentile is not the only woman in the New Testament who serves as an example of tenacious persistence in prayer. Jesus' parable of the widow and unjust judge, recorded in the eighteenth chapter of Luke, is equally familiar. You may recall that Jesus told the story of a woman who continually petitioned a certain judge for justice until he relented, even though he wasn't moral or godly. The judge's response is classic: "For some time he refused. But finally he said to himself, 'Even though I don't fear God or care what people think, yet because this widow keeps bothering me, I will see that she gets justice, so that she won't eventually come and attack me!'" (Luke 18:4–5).

The point of the Lord's story is that if, through persistence, a petitioner could move even an unkind judge, how much more should God's people be hopefully consistent in coming to a compassionate and loving Father? Jesus gives us the meaning of His story right up front, before He even tells it. In Luke 18:1, we read, "Jesus told his disciples a parable to show them that they should always pray and not give up."

Have you ever stopped and thought about the fact that Jesus prayed? Ponder that. God in human flesh, the Word of God incarnate, prayed regularly and at length. If we are ever tempted to doubt how important and necessary it is for believers to pray, we should remind ourselves of that amazing truth! And as the New Testament passages we just highlighted remind us, persistence is so important.

Of course, tenacity in asking for something that is outside of God's will isn't likely to bear much fruit, no matter how long we stay at it. Some well-meaning Christians cite Psalm 37:4—"Delight yourself in the Lord, and he will give you the desires of your heart" (ESV)—as suggesting that God will give us anything we desire. They misunderstand the truth being presented there. If we give ourselves consistently to God in prayer, spending time with Him with an open heart, He shapes and molds our desires. We begin to want the things He wants for us. When that happens, we find ourselves praying in accordance with His will for our lives. Of course, when we pray that way, amazing things can happen.

Not only in the area of prayer is persistence of more value than gold. Tenacity is a difference-making characteristic in every area of life. The brilliant French scientist Louis Pasteur said, "Let me tell you the secret that has led me to my goal: my strength lies solely in my tenacity."[2] Persistence is a powerful quality that also goes by other names, such as determination or perseverance. In recent times, another term has come into vogue: grit. This term was popularized by neuroscientist Angela Duckworth's bestselling self-help book *Grit: The Power of Passion and Perseverance.* Duckworth's book focused a well-deserved spotlight on a very biblical truth: we live in a culture obsessed with natural talent, when it is *character* that is the critical factor producing most of the great achievements in this world, particularly character traits like tenacity, or in Duckworth's vernacular, *grit.* She writes, "Enthusiasm is common. Endurance is rare."[3]

We agree. We see tenacity as a common attribute in women who make the world better and build a positive legacy. It is doubly vital, and impressive, when that tenacity is required to press through exceptional adversity or challenge. Such is the case with one of the most impactful songwriters in the history of the church.

The Incredible Persistent Legacy of Fanny Crosby

Have you ever wondered what allows a person to persist, to endure, and to keep carrying on? Sometimes when we look at someone's life through that lens, we can see the secret.

Frances Jane "Fanny" Crosby was born in 1820 in upstate New York to a family with a proud Puritan heritage and roots running back to the Mayflower pilgrims. She would grow up to be the most prolific writer of sacred songs the church has ever produced. She lived to see the twentieth century and be described as "the mother of modern congregational singing"[4] and "the Queen of Gospel Song Writers."[5] Her lyrics provided the powerful musical accompaniment for the extraordinary crusades of Dwight L. Moody. To this day, evangelical hymnals are filled with her treasured songs. In her autobiography, she noted with some pride that she was descended from Simon Crosby, one of the founders of Harvard College.

But her beginnings were troubled.

When she was just six weeks old, she got an infection that took her eyesight. Before her first birthday, her father died. Impoverished, her mother and grandmother were left with the task of providing for the family and keeping it together. To make things work, they had to move frequently, and often had to live with other people.

With those circumstances, it would have been easy for a girl to grow bitter. She was blind. Poor. Fatherless. Moving all the time, having to learn how to get around in new surroundings. What was Fanny's secret for carrying on in the midst of trial?

TENACITY COMES THROUGH GRATITUDE

Even though she lost her sight as an infant, the family held out hope for several years that some sort of medical procedure might restore her vision. By the time Fanny reached the age of five, her mother had exhausted all options. The blindness was permanent.

Fanny's "eyesight" became gratitude. She liked to say that a wonderful implication of her condition was that the first face she would ever behold would be that of her Savior when she entered heaven. So she counted herself fortunate. A remarkable gift for poetry and verse announced itself early in Fanny's life. Her first recorded poem, penned at age eight, declared,

> Oh, what a happy child I am,
> Although I cannot see!
> I am resolved that in this world

Contented I will be.
How many blessings I enjoy
That other people don't!
So weep or sigh because I'm blind,
I cannot, nor I won't![6]

This unrelenting gratitude caused her to pursue God. She had a hunger for God's Word. Beginning around age ten, with encouragement from her grandmother, Fanny memorized five chapters of the Bible each week. By fifteen, she had memorized all four gospels, the five books of Moses, Proverbs, the Song of Solomon, and many of the Psalms.

REFLECTIONS ON LEGACY

As we look at women of legacy, do you notice the common themes? Like Fanny Crosby, women of legacy all seem to face moments of trial, heartbreak, and adversity, but those moments don't break them. They continue on.

Fanny faced her challenges with cheer and a positive attitude. She chose to view her circumstances as a blessing God could use to His greater glory. She happily embraced the truths of Romans 8:28 and James 1:2—that God was working all things together for her good and that she could "count it all joy" in the face of the hardest trials.

And women of legacy turn to God's Word. This seems to be a common denominator among the women we have encountered. Women who impact the world and future generations for Christ tend to value the Bible highly and base their worldview and decisions on the principles taught in it. Fanny Crosby's unshakable faith, irrepressible optimism, and intimate familiarity with Scripture uniquely equipped her to create the soundtrack for 150 years of global evangelical growth and outreach, with the United States as its center.

TENACITY KEEPS BELIEVING IN THE CALL

Fanny was both thrilled and fascinated by the hymns she heard and sang at church, and at a very young age wondered if she might have the talent to write just one. As she began her efforts, she sensed God's favor.

Fanny's creative process always began with prayer: "I never undertake a hymn without first asking the good Lord to be my inspiration."[7] Then she would take creative cues wherever she found them. One day while helping conduct a church service at a nearby prison, she heard a shackled prisoner in the back of the room cry, "O Lord, do not pass me by."[8] That cry for mercy became the hymn "Pass Me Not, O Gentle Savior." On another occasion, a musical collaborator said he had to leave to catch a train in forty minutes and wondered if she could come up with lyrics for an entire song before he had to depart. He played a melody line for her, saying, "See if it says anything to you." To Crosby's ear the notes seemed to be whispering, "Safe in the arms of Jesus."[9] The friend left for the train station with all four verses and the chorus of that classic hymn under his arm. She once sat down to express in lyrics her own personal testimony of salvation. The result was perhaps her most famous hymn of all, "Blessed Assurance."

Many of Fanny Crosby's most beloved hymns stand among the greatest anthems of the evangelical church. These include "I Am Thine, O Lord," "Draw Me Nearer," "All the Way My Savior Leads Me," "Saved by Grace," "To God Be the Glory," and "Jesus, Keep Me Near the Cross."

Her question of writing "just" one hymn was answered. In her long and fruitful life, she crafted nearly nine thousand of them, even though she did not begin writing hymns in earnest until her forties. At the peak of her productivity, she wrote hymns under a dozen different pen names, simply to keep the majority of the songs in the most popular hymnals of the day from being authored by the same person.

That's the power of Fanny Crosby's legacy of tenacity. She persisted despite her blindness and despite all the circumstances that said she could not move forward.

Have you ever noticed that the songs you heard frequently when you were young stay burned into your memory for the rest of your life? A song can come on the radio that you haven't heard in decades, yet you can sing every word and anticipate every little musical flourish.

The same is true for me (Jackie) with many of the classic hymns of Fanny Crosby. We sang them so many times when I was a little girl growing up in church. To this day, I can sing multiple verses of many of them. That's how impressionable young minds truly are. This is especially the case with spiritual truths set to music. Once those songs are embedded, they never go away.

> Perfect submission, all is at rest,
> I in my Savior am happy and blessed,
> Watching and waiting, looking above,
> Filled with His goodness, lost in His love.[10]

Having the lyrics of wonderful classics like "Blessed Assurance" in the minds and hearts of millions is part of the extraordinary legacy of Fanny Crosby. Her life challenges us to embrace the story God gives us, to be grateful, to dig deep into His Word, and to move forward with the gifts, talents, and abilities that He has bestowed on us. There we'll find our own legacy.

Tenacity Born of Tragedy

How do you respond to life's storms, life's curveballs, tragedy?

Prior to December 3, 2011, Lauren Scruggs was a carefree Dallas-area twenty-three-year-old. She was living with her parents to save money. At the same time, she was bootstrapping a digital fashion-and-lifestyle publication called *LOLO Magazine* ("LoLo" is her nickname among close family members). A striking blonde with a big smile, Lauren possessed a real faith in Jesus Christ—a faith that was about to be tested.

A family friend invited them to ride in their private airplane to view Christmas lights above the Dallas suburbs. As she was getting off the plane, Lauren somehow was pulled into the still-spinning propeller of the aircraft. The blow instantly severed her lower left arm. Even worse, it also sliced downward through the left side of her head and face, cutting into her brain, eye, and cheek.

She remembers nothing of the incident other than waking up in the hospital days later, following multiple surgeries. As the medication wore off, she slowly began to realize that her world had changed. The physical recovery was one matter, but the emotional battle was far greater. A stern test lay ahead, including the war in her soul to come to grips with what had happened and to reconcile it with her knowledge of a God who loved her.

What young woman, even with the deepest, most mature faith, would not wrestle with questions after being suddenly injured in this way? She wrestled deeply with her identity and with questions of whether anyone could love her. Some people never return from dark places like this, but hour by hour, day by day, Lauren persisted in the fight and kept believing in God's mercy and grace.

She spoke transparently about that struggle in a 2017 interview.

> I remember just being home from the hospital. I got up one day and I felt my arm, and had the realization that this really happened. I did lose my hand. It's not a nightmare! I had this huge bandage on my eye and half of my

head is shaved, and I love beautiful hair. I remember getting into the shower and crying my eyes out. To be honest, I was in shock and I was trying to process everything that had happened. As a woman, it's natural to feel that you're losing a part of yourself. The beauty of a tragedy is that it quickly puts everything into its proper perspective. I learned in an instant that true beauty can only be found within.[11]

Perhaps that's the great message of tenacity for us all. We live in a world that loves to lift up external beauty—or for that matter, any trait that brings attention. Lauren's journey speaks of the great value of just hanging in there. By persisting, we learn, as Lauren says, that true beauty lies within. We learn to shake off the despair of the world for an enduring joy.

THE FRUIT OF TENACITY

Remember that digital magazine Lauren was attempting to launch at the time of the accident? It is now a thriving lifestyle blog drawing both a wide readership and the attention of corporate sponsors. Yet the realization of this dream represents only a sliver of Lauren's busy, purpose-filled life today.

In 2012, Lauren joined with her family to describe their journey in the widely read book *Still LoLo: A Spinning Propeller, a Horrific Accident, and a Family's Journey of Hope*. She followed its success with another book, designed to offer help and hope to others. *Your Beautiful Heart: 31 Reflections on Love, Faith, Friendship, and Becoming a Girl Who Shines* was published in 2015. And there is more.

After her accident, Lauren benefited from excellent insurance coverage that allowed her to obtain a state-of-the-art cosmetic prosthesis. She had assumed this was typical for amputees and accident victims like herself. That understanding changed in

2013, when she agreed to host a multiday event for girls who have lost limbs, called the Beautifully Flawed Retreat, conceived by Bethany Hamilton and the Friends of Bethany Hamilton foundation. You may recall that Hamilton gained worldwide notoriety after losing an arm in a shark attack while surfing at the age of thirteen.

At this event, Lauren met other young women who had suffered limb loss but disliked their unnatural-looking prosthetic limbs. Even worse, some could not obtain one at all, because the costs were simply out of reach. Many of these girls marveled at Lauren's natural-looking, silicone-covered prosthetic arm.

Touched by their ongoing emotional pain, Lauren began to pray about a way to help individuals who wanted to have a comfortable, natural-looking prosthesis but could not afford one. At the same time, she sensed a burden to provide help and support in other, less tangible ways, particularly by helping injured girls come to understand the true beauty found only in a relationship with Christ. From these concerns, in 2016 the Lauren Scruggs Kennedy Foundation, a faith-based nonprofit organization, was born.

One of the biggest fears Lauren faced in the immediate aftermath of her accident was related to her dreams of marriage and family. In her darkest hours, her inner voice whispered that this attack on her external beauty meant that she would never be loved by the kind of man she had always dreamed of meeting. Nevertheless, with God's help she tenaciously fought through those fears and began a series of very public appearances in support of her first book.

One of these was a 2013 interview—less than two years removed from her accident—with Giuliana Rancic on the *E! News* television program. After the interview, Giuliana told Lauren she needed to meet her *E! News* cohost Jason Kennedy. Lauren and Jason chatted, and that first meeting sparked a friendship that quickly grew to romance. He would later write of meeting Lauren, "This was someone *real*. At the time, Lauren was in the thick of recovery, facing insecurities and uncertainties—but she was finding the confidence to put herself out there because she knew it could help others. You couldn't miss how beautiful that was . . . And even from across the studio, I noticed her smile . . . After such a terrible accident, Lauren could have chosen *not* to smile and to view the world with bitterness and pain. And yet she was smiling. I wanted to get to know the woman behind that smile."[12]

Jason did get to know Lauren, and the following May he flew to Dallas, secretly filled her apartment with white tulips, and spelled out "Will you marry me?" in candles on the lawn below her balcony.

Lauren said yes. The next December, in a celebrity-studded ceremony at the Dallas Four Seasons hotel—covered wire to wire by *People* and *Us* magazine, and of course *E! News*—the two were married. They now make their home in Studio City, California, to be close to Jason's television work. Lauren divides her time between her online magazine, her foundation, and promoting a new dry shampoo line she named Stranded. A portion of the profits supports her charity.

She continues to build her life on a foundation of faith in God and honor for His Word. She reminds herself and others of the scriptural exhortation in Proverbs 31:30: "Charm is deceptive, and beauty is fleeting; but a woman who fears the LORD is to be praised."

She has said, "I think that stands as the foundation of my life, as God is never changing. Our outward beauty is constantly changing as is everything in the world, but God's love for us is always there and always comforting. God is everything. God is hope and encouragement for others. To me, that's true beauty. Beauty is what's inside of you."[13]

Beauty is what's inside of you—we love that! And that beauty can manifest itself in so many ways. I (Jackie) think about my daughter-in-law Erica. In the middle of her own busy life, raising four children and having a husband who travels a lot, Erica has made time to serve single mothers in her church. Each year, she has helped coordinate a day on which the church shows love and support to this group of mothers by providing childcare, spa treatments, and car repairs. It's a wonderful way to express care and concern and bring out the beauty in others. Simple acts of service are something we can all do. Our aim is to be faithful with what God puts in front of us. Sometimes the fruit of our tenacity is simply to be found faithful in this life and to hear the words of our heavenly Father in the next life: "Well done." That's an encouraging, challenging otherworldly perspective.

My Legacy Reflections

For me (Lauren), tenacity is often easy to identify in others, but how do you know whether you have it yourself? What does it look like to live out grit and persistence personally? I haven't always been able to give voice to what this looks like, except to say it is a day-to-day decision, with a long-term vision for what is possible.

I am sure that if we could sit down with any of the women highlighted here while they were in the thick of things, they would confess to the same kinds of moments of doubt and hopelessness, the same temptation to give up, that you and I experience. I'm convinced that tenacity grows when we walk through those moments and come out on the other side with hope, because we know we are not alone, and we know the end of our story.

I believe there is another key to cultivating tenacity: an eternal perspective. Look with fresh eyes at Hebrews 12:2, which says, ". . . fixing our eyes on Jesus, the pioneer and perfecter of faith. For the joy set before him he endured the cross, scorning its shame, and sat down at the right hand of the throne of God."

Wow! Did you catch it? It was for the joy Christ saw ahead of Him that He endured the cross. Christ knew what the end of the story was. He knew there was victory and life on the other side of that cross. This pulled Him through the most difficult trial anyone ever endured.

It is usually wise to take the long view when making decisions. And there is no view longer than eternity. When I remember Christ is with me, and I know the victory I have through Him, it makes the challenges of this world more bearable. It gives me strength to keep moving forward, to carry on through adversity, in the hope of making this world better by glorifying God with my "only one life."

Even now, though I'm still only in my twenties, I see the benefit of the long view. I started work at Hobby Lobby straight out of college, got married, and started working on my master's (which turned into a second master's degree). I know all that sounds crazy, and it was a turbulent time. But to know that those seasons aren't forever makes all the difference. Eventually, the waters calm and we can look back and say, "Wow, look what God did!" Of course, I've now entered another challenging season, since my PhD work and my day job are both even more intense. (Whew! I'm glad I had this chapter to remind me to persevere!)

There is a third key that I believe tends to produce the kind of grit that keeps you going when you're tempted to quit. You see, whether we realize it or not, we all base our decisions on our values. What we value orders our priorities.

Is this a yes or is this a no? Do I quit or do I keep going? The answer you come up with is a result of what you value. Allow me to put it another way: conviction is what produces tenacity. Donatiya, the Syrophoenician woman, valued her daughter's healing above doing what was considered proper for a woman of her status, and she persisted at all costs to procure that healing. Fanny Crosby valued Christ above her sight and above her self-pity. In joy, she persevered in writing thousands of hymns to help others see spiritual truth. Lauren Scruggs Kennedy valued hope, so she refused to give up during what seemed a hopeless situation. Instead she kept fighting so that she and countless others could find true beauty from within.

What are your core convictions? Whatever they are, you are more likely to be gritty and persistent in the pursuit of those beliefs. And the stronger those convictions, the greater your tenacity. To remind myself of these ideas, I find myself turning to Romans 5:3–5: "We also glory in our sufferings, because we know that suffering produces perseverance; perseverance, character; and character, hope. And hope does not put us to shame, because God's love has been poured out into our hearts through the Holy Spirit, who has been given to us." Suffering, perseverance, character, and hope—they all go together. This is not like Monopoly, in which we get to pass Go and go straight to hope. Hope comes through tenacity.

You've been given one life. It will soon be past. Have you allowed God's Word to influence your values and convictions? As you do, you'll be fiercely tenacious about the things that matter most.

CHAPTER 10

THE LEGACY OF FAITH

*Faith sees the invisible, believes the
unbelievable, and receives the impossible.*

—Corrie ten Boom[1]

aith is the belief that the impossible is possible. It is what enables us to hope and face difficult days with peace. The Scriptures speak encouragingly to people who exercise faith: "God is not ashamed to be called their God, for he has prepared a city for them" (Heb. 11:16). When we think about great women of faith, is there any better place to start than Mary of Nazareth?

Faith in the Impossible

There is sometimes a faith that costs you everything yet gains you everything. Such is the way of faith in the impossible. Such is the faith of Mary. She exercised faith in the little decisions and the big moments alike, as well as everything in between. We're thinking particularly of one occasion involving wine, a wedding, and a mother's fierce faith.

EXERCISING FAITH IN THE LITTLE THINGS

It's a crisis. There is a wedding in the village of Cana, a big occasion in most cultures but especially so among the Jews of first-century Galilee. The event can run for days, as members of the extended family travel great distances to attend and celebrate. Now, at the culmination of the festivities, the family has run out of wine.

This is no small faux pas or inconvenience. It is not only humiliating for the family; there is a deeply rooted tradition that suggests it is an inauspicious beginning for the union. Once the depletion of the wine is announced, many of the guests will believe this portends a bad future for the couple. Thus the despair of the mother of the groom.

Mary and some of her adult children are in attendance. So when she learns of her friend's dire predicament, she locates her eldest—Y'Shua in Hebrew, Jesus in Greek—and pulls Him into a back room of the house, where food is being prepared.

She is confident that her son can somehow, in some way, remedy this tragic social embarrassment. Of course, this will require a miracle, which Jesus has never performed in public. Nevertheless, she displays an unshakeable faith that all He has to do is give a command and her friend's problem will be solved.

After some initial reluctance, the command will be given, and the water in numerous large, ceremonial stone pots will be instantly transformed into roughly 180 gallons of the finest wine any of the guests has ever tasted.

This is no great test of her faith. She can believe Him for the little things because she's believed in the big things. And that's no small lesson to learn: how we need to exercise faith in even our day-to-day events, trials, ups and downs!

EXERCISING FAITH IN THE BIG THINGS

Mary knows her son is special. She has known it since before He was conceived. The real test came on that day thirty-one years ago when the impending conception had been announced to her by an angelic visitor. She was young, innocent, and betrothed to a good man from the village when the archangel Gabriel appeared to her and announced that she would soon be with child. His message carried news that was even more astonishing: "You are to call him Jesus. He will be great and will be called the Son of the Most High. The Lord God will give him the throne of his father David, and he will reign over Jacob's descendants forever; his kingdom will never end" (Luke 1:31–33).

The appearance of an angelic messenger was stunning enough, but the message he delivered was a thousand times more extraordinary. She immediately recognized the implications of the phrases "throne of David" and "reign over Jacob's descendants." He was saying she would give birth to Israel's long-awaited Messiah.

This report challenged Mary's faith at two profound and fundamental levels. First, did she believe the message was true? Second, if she did, it would mean revealing a pregnancy while she was still betrothed. That would be a horrific scandal. Mary knew this. It would cost her everything. Her marriage would never be looked on in favor, and her child would always be "that boy"! How could she look her parents in the face? She would be an outcast.

Her faith gave her the strength to look past the present problem and focus on the miracle. In response to the angel's proclamation, the young girl posed a simple, single question: "How can this be, since I am a virgin?"

The angel responded with three assurances—that the conception would be a work of the Holy Spirit, that God's power would overshadow her protectively, and that as a sign, she would soon learn that her elderly, barren cousin Elizabeth was great with child. Each would be an impossibility in Mary's mind and in her own experience. Again her faith stretched to include this mystery.

Her reply to the angel is striking. She declared herself to be the servant of the Lord and added, "May it be done to me according to your word."

And so it was.

Thirty-three years later, her faith will once again be tried in the extreme. She will stand on a barren, rocky outcrop on the edge of Jerusalem and take in the sight of that same eldest son dying cruelly on a cross. With all but a couple of her son's followers scattered and in hiding, she will stand with Him in His darkest hour. She will hear His final words. Among them will be instructions to His closest friend concerning her care and well-being.

Mary's extraordinary life and remarkable faith made her a vital part of God's successful plan to bring the Redeemer into the world. Legacies do not get any bigger than that. Have you ever wondered what would have happened if Mary had refused to believe? Her faith teaches us much today. She believed in the impossible (a virgin birth) because she believed that God was limitless. Is it any wonder that when something simple came up, like running out of wine, she knew Jesus could handle it? She believed in Him. She trusted in the seemingly impossible. How we need to learn and live out that kind of faith every day!

As we have repeatedly emphasized in these pages, you have only one life to live. By cultivating and growing your faith, you will ensure that your life and legacy have an impact on others long after your time on earth is over. You will have an opportunity to affect people in a memorable way. Your beliefs influence your values; your values influence your actions.

Faith is like a muscle. It needs exercise. This isn't glamorous. Being a person of faith is frequently the opposite of glamorous. And it certainly isn't modern or sophisticated. The gospel story we have based our lives on is twenty centuries old, and so simple that a child of five or six can comprehend it. Yet it is the most powerful thing a human being can grasp. And most of us received the faith that defines our lives at the knees of a woman, most often a mother.

This truth reminds us of a story that lies behind a familiar old saying. Around 1865, the American poet William Ross Wallace, the son of a Scottish Presbyterian minister, found himself in a late-night philosophical conversation with a group of other artist friends. The subject under debate? "What rules the world?"

Impassioned cases were made for military might, political prowess, wealth, scientific technology, and other forces. Wallace listened silently to the discussion for a bit and then dismissed himself. He returned a short time later holding a sheet of paper on which he had jotted several verses of a new poem with the title "What Rules the World?" Each stanza concluded with the same lines:

> For the hand that rocks the cradle
> Is the hand that rules the world.

Wallace understood a truth the others had overlooked—that the fate of nations and the course of history is determined by people who shape the character and worldviews of future leaders when they are very young. Unseen behind the names in the news headlines and history book titles are women who rocked the cradles, read the bedtime stories, and explained the world to those history makers when their minds and hearts were impressionable.

In Victorian-era Great Britain, this power was vested not only in mothers but also, among the British upper classes, in nannies as well.

The Hand of Faith That Rocked the World

Elizabeth Anne Everest was born to humble circumstances in 1832. She died penniless while living with her sister. She never married, and she remains essentially unknown except to a handful of historians and history buffs.

Yet her influence on the twentieth century cannot be overstated.

It can be argued that because of her, the Nazis did not come to rule Europe, and because of the way she carried out her duties, the Soviets would not realize their aspirations to extend their brand of Communism to the world.

CULTIVATING FAITH

As a single person, Elizabeth accepted her status in life and chose to care for children. In the first phase of her career, she served as a nanny for an Anglican minister, Reverend Thompson Phillips, and his wife. This in spite of the fact that Mrs. Everest (nannies were customarily referred to as "Mrs." whether married or not) was not a member of the Church of England but rather a fiercely devout "low church" believer.

As a low church Christian, she embraced an evangelistic, revivalistic expression of faith that emphasized a direct, personal relationship with God through prayer, conversion, and Bible study focused on personal application of scriptural principles. These "nonconformists," as they were sometimes called, included Congregationalists, Baptists, Methodists, Presbyterians, and others. Low church strains of Christianity were in contrast with "high church" strains, which were marked by liturgy and ornate ceremony—specifically, Roman Catholicism and, in Britain, the Church of England, or the Anglican Church.

With a solid faith, Elizabeth Everest cared for Reverend and Mrs. Phillips's daughter, Ella, for twelve years, until her services were no longer needed. It is easy to imagine that caring for the only child of a gentle Anglican minister was not an overly arduous assignment. The same could not be said for her next mission. In 1875, her new assignment would prove to be more challenging than she could possibly have imagined.

EXERCISING FAITH FAITHFULLY

The infant boy who became her charge would, in a few years, be labeled by tactful souls as "quite difficult" and by more blunt observers as "a little monster." Growing up small of stature, somewhat sickly, and with a speech impediment, Winston, the firstborn son of Lord Randolph Churchill, was not viewed by his father, or anyone else who knew him, as a prospect for future greatness—or even future mediocrity. His father seems to have believed his son had some sort of mental deficiency.

Throughout his childhood, the sole exception to this gloomy prediction remained Mrs. Everest. She came to recognize that the little boy possessed a remarkable but unconventional intellect and that he was starving for parental love and validation he would never receive.

Churchill's father and mother were the stereotype of emotionally detached Victorian parents, but they carried this to the extreme. Both, fiercely ambitious to climb higher on the ladder of British society, displayed little affection for, or even interest in, Winston or his younger brother, Jack, who came along a few years later. What attention Winston did receive from his father was negative and critical. The man openly speculated that his lisping, distracted, high-strung son was "retarded." Winston's son, Randolph, later wrote that "the neglect and lack of interest in him shown by his parents were remarkable, even judged by the standards of late Victorian and Edwardian days."[2]

"Woom," as Winston began calling Mrs. Everest when he was too small to correctly pronounce *woman*, was his sole source of emotional support and encouragement for the first two decades of his life. He would later write, "I loved my mother dearly—but at a distance. My nurse was my confidante. Mrs. Everest it was who looked after me and tended all my wants. It was to her I poured out all my many troubles."[3]

Elizabeth Everest provided far more than comfort for the lonely, anguished little boy. She lovingly but firmly enforced boundaries that ultimately calmed him down and helped him focus.

But Elizabeth not only taught young Winston self-discipline; she *discipled* him in an authentic Christian faith. She was the woman who modeled and taught the boy the value and power of exercising faith, a personal faith. Author Stephen Mansfield wrote of Everest, "She helped him memorize his first Scriptures, knelt with him daily as he recited his prayers, and explained the world to him in simple but distinctly Christian terms . . . Years later, when he was under fire on some remote battlefield or entangled in the most troubling difficulties, he found himself praying the prayers he had learned at Mrs. Everest's knee."[4]

Churchill was sent away to boarding school at the age of eight and was miserable there. Bullied by both teachers and upperclassmen, consistently scoring at or near the bottom of his class, he was near despair. He was also homesick. He wrote his parents repeatedly, pleading with them to come visit him. They never came. Yet Mrs. Everest did.

This relationship was deep and powerful. Throughout his eventful adult life, right up until his death, it was not a picture of his parents that sat on Churchill's nightstand but a beloved photo of Mrs. Everest.

As a young man, Winston briefly, outwardly, seemed to wander from the biblical faith he absorbed at Mrs. Everest's knee, flirting instead with the scientific rationalism so much in vogue at that moment in history. At the turn of the twentieth century, science seemed to offer mankind the promise of unlimited progress. This was before the horrors of two world wars, a holocaust, and the Cold War's threat of nuclear annihilation shattered these illusions.

Nevertheless, after Winston became a young officer in the

British cavalry, his faith reemerged, providing comfort and strength in times of danger or extreme stress. Churchill's first time under direct fire came in Cuba when he was only twenty-one, and after that experience, while visiting a friend in New York, he received word that Mrs. Everest had fallen gravely ill. It is poignantly telling that, on hearing of her condition, Churchill rushed back to England and stayed at her side for the final week of her life. "She was my favourite friend," he recorded in his journal after her passing.

ELIZABETH'S ENDURING LEGACY OF FAITH

Later in life, when Churchill would write of his many harrowing experiences as a correspondent and soldier, he would attest that the prayers and spiritual principles he had absorbed from Elizabeth Everest were the anchor of his soul. He prayed fervently for help and guidance during each ordeal, and when he came through unscathed, under near-miraculous circumstances, he was confident that his deliverance was evidence of answered prayer.

Elizabeth Everest gave Winston Churchill more than a personal faith that could sustain him in trying times and fuel a sense of divine purpose. She also gave him something else: a Christian worldview.

God used the faith of an obscure woman of humble origins to shape the character of one of history's key figures. Would Britain have weathered the Nazi firestorm of the Battle of Britain without Churchill's spine-stiffening oratory? It is doubtful. Would the democratic West have resisted Communist expansionism and outlasted the Soviet Union without Churchill's early, prescient warnings? Perhaps not.

Oh, how different the story of the twentieth century would be had Mrs. Elizabeth Everest not been a woman of legacy through faith.

At the very beginning of this book, we pointed out how Marie Green imparted her faith and values to my (Jackie's) father-in-law, David Green, and to all of his siblings. Clearly, the hand that rocked the cradle in that modest little parsonage understood the immense power and responsibility that mothers and caregivers of children wield.

There is nothing more important than to point a child toward their Heavenly Father and the redemption available through Christ. We are instructed in many places in the Bible to teach God's words to our children and to our children's children so they don't forget to love the Lord, walk in his ways, and hold fast to him (Deut. 11:19–22). In doing so, we help that child form a Christian worldview. We live in the midst of a generation in which many Christians, although they love God, don't have a worldview that aligns with their professed faith. Women of strength and biblical knowledge can change this, and in so doing, raise up Winston Churchills for a new generation.

Our Journey of Faith: A Museum

We never thought we'd be part of opening a museum. But that's what faith does. It takes us on great adventures that we'd never choose to go on ourselves.

THE JOURNEY BEGINS

Around 2007, a group approached Hobby Lobby president Steve Green—my (Jackie's) husband and my (Lauren's) father—seeking donor funding for a special project. They had a vision for a Bible-centric museum or exhibit in Dallas, Texas, and they came with a proposal that Hobby Lobby help them acquire a building somewhere in the Dallas-Fort Worth metropolitan area.

Steve conferred with the family, and we all saw merit in the concept. Steve and I (Jackie) had many late-night conversations about the magnitude of the project and what it would mean, although none of us could have fully anticipated what the coming months and years would hold. I had my doubts, but the project was certainly in alignment with our core passions and values. Not to mention the expertise that Steve had available to him in evaluating and acquiring real estate. So a search began in Dallas for an appropriate building to purchase on behalf of this group that had a passion and a dream.

As it happened, nearly two years of searching, and numerous trips from Oklahoma City to Dallas, proved fruitless. Several prospective properties were considered, but there was never a good alignment of structure, location, and price. Much of this journey is chronicled in our book *This Dangerous Book: How the Bible Has Shaped Our World and Why It Still Matters Today* (Zondervan, 2017).

The group returned with another proposal. A very rare and extraordinary fragment of the New Testament, on purple vellum, was being placed on the market by a collector in Istanbul, Turkey. The men wanted to know if there would be an interest in buying it and donating it to their planned exhibit. There was indeed an interest, and in the fall of 2009, the process of potentially acquiring it began.

While we did not end up purchasing that particular artifact, God was preparing us for a much bigger plan. We began learning about the science and the economics of ancient Bible manuscripts and fragments. As it turns out, that world is a specialized, tight-knit community. Word spread quickly that an American business was in the market to purchase rare and ancient biblical artifacts. Soon potential sellers came out of the woodwork.

Since that first acquisition did not pan out, we set about seeing if we might be able to acquire a different piece. We did find one. Buying that one led to viewing and buying another. And another. And still others followed. We were fascinated because each manuscript we bought represented a precious piece of church history. I was able to go on some of these early trips with Steve. It was truly exciting, and of course, because Lauren was working for the museum at the time, she got to see each new artifact as it was acquired.

Each manuscript or volume we encountered was a thread in the ancient, colorful tapestry that is the story of our miraculous Bible. As we followed the path we found ourselves on, we began sensing a heart and calling to share that story. In the process, a vision for something much larger and more ambitious began to come into focus: a national museum of the Bible. It also was increasingly clear that what God wanted to bring into existence was certainly bigger than anyone had originally imagined.

Within two short years, we found ourselves in possession of what one magazine article described as "one of the world's largest private collections of rare biblical texts and artifacts."[5] Each purchase was a step of faith. The more of these treasures we encountered, the more convinced our family became that each artifact's story—the Bible's story—needed to be shared with the world and not stay locked away in vaults, largely unknown.

QUESTIONING YOUR FAITH

It's easy to look back now and see how God's plan was unfolding, but as we were on the journey, the trail was misty, clouded, and uncertain. At times, we were tempted to question God's intentions, but mostly our ability to carry His plan through to fruition. Quite frankly, I found myself asking God, "Don't you have someone better to send down this path?" At this point in the journey, we had to stop and consider what God was doing. It was evident that He was opening the doors.

It seemed pretty clear that God was drawing us into the world of ancient artifacts, manuscripts, and a Bible museum. What had started as an idea soon became a stewardship responsibility and eventually felt more like a calling to complete with the highest standard possible.

The only thing that really qualified us, as a family, to oversee the creation of a world-class collection of ancient Bible manuscripts and a center for Bible research was our common reverence for the Book. God's Word has not only been the foundation of our personal lives; it has been the compass by which we steered our business. What is more, throughout the years, much of our charitable giving has been directed toward institutions and organizations that teach or champion the Bible.

Yet we know it is the way of our God to scramble up qualification and calling. He called Peter, the rustic fisherman from Galilee, to be Christ's ambassador to the elite Jewish establishment in Jerusalem. At the same time, He sent Paul, the scholar with the impeccable Jewish pedigree, to share the gospel with a Gentile businesswoman in Philippi.

While I'd had the opportunity to participate in much of the family's charitable giving activities, this was one of the first in which I felt a sense of personal calling. That reality was both invigorating and frightening. I felt unqualified, and I knew there would be a cost—more travel for me and time away from home.

It seems God has built this world in such a way that acts that carry eternal significance always require faith. This is why following Christ in obedience continually pulls us out of our comfort zones. If God called us to do things that came naturally and easily to us, we would constantly fall into the trap of self-sufficiency, trying to accomplish them in our own strength. We wouldn't be dependent on Him and His grace. We laugh because we know that if God had given us a glimpse of the true scope, size, and complexity of this project, we might not have had the faith to see it through. We have said many times that God lets you know what you need to know, when you need to know it. So we pressed ahead in faith, obedient to follow His lead into the unknown.

A NEXT STEP OF FAITH: A TRAVELING EXHIBIT

The vision for the museum was still developing when Steve came up with the idea of a traveling exhibition. We were excited to be able to share the treasures of Bible history that over the centuries only a handful of people had glimpsed. We wanted as many people as possible—believers and non-Christians alike—to appreciate the sacrifices and providential miracles that brought us all the English-language Bible we take for granted. Our goal was to bring to life the story of the Bible's integrity through preservation.

We called this exhibit *Passages* and timed the launch in our home base of Oklahoma City in May of 2011 to coincide with the four hundredth anniversary of the completion of the iconic King James Bible. This stretched our faith as well. The creation of a world-class traveling exhibition was no small undertaking. *Passages* covered fifteen thousand square feet of space and featured animatronic characters, interactive displays, immersive experiences, and of course more than four hundred rare and rarely-before-seen biblical artifacts. Following the initial exhibit in Oklahoma City, museum exhibits like *Passages* traveled the world, making stops that included many colleges and universities and even the Vatican. It is estimated that more than half a million people worldwide have experienced a Museum of the Bible traveling exhibit.

The creation of *Passages* served as valuable preparation for the next, even more ambitious, phase of this calling. We knew early on that we wanted to create a permanent home for an expanded version of the exhibit, one that could also serve as a leading center of academic research and study of ancient Bible manuscripts. Our initial thoughts were that Dallas or New York City might be suitable homes for such a museum, but eventually we were drawn to the heart of Washington, D.C., the site of many of the nation's most important museums, and a place where hundreds of thousands of schoolchildren and families visit each year. This, of course, would require the biggest leap of faith we'd ever felt impressed to undertake.

We found a building a mere two blocks from the historic National Mall and three blocks from the US Capitol, providing 430,000 square feet of space for exhibits, lecture halls, research labs, archival libraries, a virtual flyboard ride that takes you throughout D.C., a 472-seat performance theatre, special interactive places for children and families, a recreation of the village of Nazareth, and even a rooftop garden.

As a family, we generally shy away from talking about money, particularly where our charitable giving or philanthropy is concerned, but needless to say, the scope of this project has demanded an enormous investment of both money and time. Early on, our commitment was to provide half the funding for this undertaking and to pray for other donors who would take hold of the vision for the project and partner with us for the other half. This stretched our faith farther than we thought possible. What if no one was willing to contribute? Yet we had experienced God's faithfulness at every turn up to that point in the process. We believed with all our hearts we were following His will and purpose. So we kept moving forward.

In the fall of 2010, the initial planning for the traveling exhibit *Passages* began. Then in 2012, an amazing location for what would become the Museum of the Bible was acquired. Construction started in 2014, and three years later, in November of 2017, the eight-story, world-class, one-of-a-kind facility opened its doors to the public.

As we said previously, had we known at the outset the magnitude of what God was calling us to and the demands it would make on us in terms of time, travel, prayer, and work, we might have turned and run the other direction. However, we can say two things with confidence. It was worth it. And it was God who made it happen. Only He could have pulled off something like this. We're just not that clever, but we do try to be available. And in reality, that is all God is looking for from any of us. The eyes of the Lord search to and fro throughout the earth for people who will simply trust and be fully committed to Him. He is looking for faith.

MY EXERCISE OF FAITH

Back in the fall of 2009, just as the vision for the Museum of the Bible was beginning to emerge, I (Lauren) was in my final year of college at the University of Oklahoma. Like most seniors, I was already looking past graduation in May and wondering what came next.

I had been working part-time at Hobby Lobby since the age of sixteen. Still, after some prayer and soul searching, I determined that I wanted to see if there might be an opportunity for me at the corporate office. You might be surprised to learn that, even for the daughter of the company's president, there was no guarantee of such an opportunity. Even though we are a close-knit family with a family-owned business, Hobby Lobby's policy has always been that family members aren't entitled to a job. They have to qualify just like every other applicant, and they have to start at the bottom. I expressed my desire to my father, and he agreed to be on the lookout for a position that might be a good fit for my experience, skills, and degree.

By the time the spring semester rolled around, the acquisition of biblical artifacts and manuscripts was really accelerating. So much so that there was a need for someone to curate and catalog all items. As it happened, my degree program in classics and letters made me a good fit for just such a task. Before I even graduated, I began working part-time cataloging and indexing the many pieces being added to the collection. Upon graduation, I transitioned to a full-time position. Before long, I was managing a busy team of twelve curators and registrars, most of whom had advanced academic degrees.

As I've mentioned previously, I don't necessarily enjoy being in the spotlight. So working with my team all day in an archival warehouse facility was a comfortable situation for me. Of course, I was surrounded by incredibly smart, very educated people, and I was this fresh-faced, wide-eyed kid just out of college. Yet I found that in my perceived weakness, God was strong in me. I think this was what the Lord was getting at when He told the apostle Paul, "My grace is sufficient for you, for my power is made perfect in weakness" (2 Cor. 12:9).

I would continue to need that power, because after a few years, I transitioned to being the museum's director of community engagement. At that time, the key focus was raising the other half of the funds needed to build and equip the Museum of the Bible. Naturally, this involved reaching out to families and foundations that might have a heart for the project. I went from being hidden away in a warehouse to spending my days talking to strangers, speaking publicly, and making presentations. At first I was overwhelmed, and I had my share of stumbles, but each day, little by little, I found my courage growing. I still have a way to go, but I'm encouraged by the progress.

Does anything carry more legacy-building power than faith in God? Faith not only transforms everything about the individual but also influences everyone around them. Here is an even more stunning thought: faith carries multigenerational influence. Is it possible that your ancestors have had a far greater impact on who you are and what God calls you to do than you realize? We certainly began to think so when, while doing some research on our genealogy, we discovered a remarkable woman of legacy in the branches of our family tree. And that discovery ended up connecting to the Museum of the Bible in an amazing way!

As I've (Jackie) mentioned, for my birthday a few years ago, my husband, Steve, blessed me with a most wonderful and unusual present. He gifted me the services of a professional genealogist to map out our family history. He knew that I had already become semi-obsessed with this subject after subscribing to one of the popular online genealogy research services.

I had been on several trips with my grandmother, mother, and aunts to search for more information on our family tree. My grandmother and mother recalled many stories that my great-grandmother had shared about our family line tracing back to George Washington and royalty in England. These trips just made me want to know more about our family history.

As I mentioned in chapter 4, through this whole process I discovered that Queen Elizabeth II is my ninth cousin. I was delighted to also learn that my family line extends back even farther to the first Queen Elizabeth, who reigned from 1558 to 1603.

The discovery came about one day back in 2016 as I was sharing some of these genealogical revelations with one of the brilliant collection curators on our staff. In response, he said, "Well, if you're related to Queen Elizabeth, I think there's a good chance you might also be related to Elizabeth de Bohun, the English noblewoman connected to the remarkable new manuscript we just received!"

Looking at the exciting details, I found out that this ancestor of mine (her name is pronounced "deh-boon"), who illustrated the manuscript *The Hours and Psalter of Elizabeth de Bohun*, was part of a family of extremely devout Christians who used their wealth to commission beautiful works of art. Some of the finest manuscripts of the fourteenth century were commissioned by Elizabeth's family, including her in-laws.

As a matter of fact, *The Hours and Psalter of Elizabeth de Bohun* was at one time a centerpiece of the private collection of William Waldorf Astor, the richest man in America at the end of the nineteenth century. In 1883, Astor loaned this and other pieces from his collection to an exhibition in New York to help raise funds to provide a pedestal for the Statue of Liberty. At the time, the *Chicago Tribune* called it "the grandest 14th Century English manuscript in private hands."[6]

What a beautiful moment! I had suddenly discovered that one of the most important and exciting manuscripts in our large and growing collection was connected to *my* ancestor! That can't possibly be an accident or coincidence. It served as a small but gratifying sign that there were threads of faith in my family's tapestry that were being woven throughout time unbeknownst to me, yet I was able to appreciate the fruits of their investment. And the gift of legacy was clear, right in front of me. Elizabeth de Bohun lived only a brief life, yet here we are seven centuries later talking about her and how her/my family invested in the Word of God. She and her husband commissioned this beautifully illustrated manuscript—at great financial expense—during a time when there was much unrest in England and much of the population could not read. The same faith that compelled them to create these beautiful works built around Scripture has flowed down through the centuries, right down to me, as a living legacy.

The museum journey produced a thousand points of growth for Lauren and me. Every grand opening of a *Passages* exhibit produced a new (and stretching) speaking opportunity. Every step of construction produced groundbreaking ceremonies, hard hat tours of the building, events designed to build awareness, fundraising galas, and ultimately an entire series of grand opening events. Each was an opportunity to speak, meet people, and engage them in the mission.

Along the way, something curious happened. At so many of the events, women would come up to me and ask all sorts of questions, like, "How do you balance it all?" "How can I be involved?" or "How did you discover your passion?" The underlying theme of those heartfelt conversations was always the same: each of those women realized that they had only one life—one life to do something of impact, to be part of something meaningful and lasting. They also wanted to share their legacy with others and promote what was foundational in their lives—their faith and the Bible. And that's when the seeds for this book began to form. I realized that so many women needed the encouragement and inspiration to be legacy builders as well. So often, as women, we yearn to do something meaningful, yet we fail to see the everyday opportunities right before our eyes.

As a result of these conversations, Lauren and I began gathering women for what we called Women of Legacy events. These events became a time to encourage women to be legacy builders, whether their legacy was big or small. We are still learning, but our Women of Legacy events are becoming regular occurrences, and we've found a real source of inspiration as we tell women, "You can leave a legacy too!" God can use *anybody* to do great things! All it takes is faith that no matter who you are or where you are, we all serve the same powerful God. He is just looking for people who will boldly trust Him and say yes. May we step out in faith in God's promises and say, just as Mary did, "I am the Lord's servant. . . . May your word to me be fulfilled" (Luke 1:38).

CHAPTER 11

THE LEGACY OF PRAYER

*As prayer warriors, we must remember
that no matter how hopeless a situation
may appear to us, God gives us power in
prayer to do something about it. We may be
overwhelmed by it, but God isn't. We may not
see a way out, but God can.*

—Stormie Omartian[1]

Prayer may well leave the greatest legacy. How many great acts would never have been performed, how many great endeavors would never have been undertaken, how many great people would never have been inspired, were it not for someone's prayers? Prayer is almost always done in private and viewed by no one, but God in His divine wisdom sometimes allows us to see the *impact* of our prayers.

When a Prayer Is a Promise

Hannah's sun-weathered, time-creviced face breaks into a smile as a passing neighbor inquires about her famous son, the prophet-judge, the most significant individual in all of Israel. She beams, not just with pride but also with rays of gratitude and joy, as she relays the latest news about her miracle boy, Samuel. "Of course, I pray for him every day," she tells her friend.

Hannah is a person who prays often. Two pivotal prayers define her life, standing like sacred pillars holding up a remarkable story of God's faithfulness and love.

She uttered both of these prayers in nearby Shiloh, the holy location of the tabernacle of the Lord. There resides the ark of the covenant, and the high priest Eli, a direct descendant of Aaron. And it was there that, driven by desperation, she first boldly entered the outer court of the habitation of God in order to plead her case to the holy Judge of Judges.

A PLEADING PRAYER

Hannah's smile melts away when she recalls the heartache and shame of the time prior to that first prayer. Her childless years. Barrenness in her culture carries more than social stigma; it can be catastrophic economically. Wives outlive their husbands, and childless widows often end up begging in the street. Compounding her agony back then were the prideful taunts of her husband's other wife. That woman had borne Elkanah numerous children and never skipped an opportunity to rub that in Hannah's face.

After years of relentless disappointment and frustration, Hannah decided to use the family's annual pilgrimage to Shiloh to seek the intervention of her heavenly Father. After the evening meal, Hannah knelt before the Lord and went to battle with a fierceness fueled by righteous indignation.

The thought of her ancient forefather Abraham crossed her mind in this moment of contending. Hadn't he been blessed with a miracle son? And hadn't he, in faith and devotion, been willing to offer him up to the Lord? So as she silently prayed, she offered her miracle son up in advance of his conception.

Oh, God, if You will bless me with a son, I will dedicate him to Your holy service.

She prayed with such intensity, mouthing the words to her

prayer but making no sound, that the high priest Eli, watching unseen from the doorway of the tabernacle, thought her intoxicated. Just a moment of conversation with the devout woman convinced him otherwise. Moved by her faith and fervency, the only mortal on earth authorized to enter the Holy of Holies and minister in the manifest presence of God spoke a blessing of fulfillment over Hannah. "Go in peace!" he said. "May the God of Israel grant the request you have asked of Him."

All these years later, Hannah still remembers how her faith soared to hear those words from the man of God. Not a flicker of doubt remained in her heart from that moment. Her feet scarcely touched the ground as she rushed back to her husband. As the chronicles of Israel will record for all time, nine months later she held an infant son in her arms. She named him Samuel, which means "requested of God."

Requested and granted.

A PRAYER OF DEDICATION

Then there was that second milestone prayer. When the boy was fully weaned—at roughly two years old—she and her husband faithfully made good on Hannah's sacred promise. Together they took Samuel back to Shiloh and to Eli. There they offered him in the lifelong service of the Lord, as a ward of the high priest and the tabernacle. Before she left, though, Hannah had another prayer to offer. The previous prayer in this spot had been one of desperate longing. On this day, though, her lips produced an anthem of victory and gratitude.

> "My heart rejoices in the Lord!
>   The Lord has made me strong.
> Now I have an answer for my enemies;
>   I rejoice because you rescued me.
> No one is holy like the Lord!

> There is no one besides you;
> there is no Rock like our God."

All these years later, an aged Hannah's smile returns as she ponders the wonders of a faithful God, the gracious One whose ear inclines to the cries of a heartsick woman and is moved by her faith. Here's the beauty of Scripture. God gives us a powerful glimpse of Hannah's anguished prayer.

Samuel will go on to become one of the most beloved judges in all the history of Israel. Like Hannah, he has a spirit sensitive to the voice of God. He will appoint Israel's first king, Saul. He will later appoint King David as a replacement for Saul. Through the house of David, the Redeemer will ultimately arise. All these events will be the fruit of one woman's fervent prayer.

Prayer. It is God's great invitation. So many times in the Scriptures, we see the example of praying people. And equally important, we see God's appeal to us to pray. As we mentioned in chapter 9, Jesus illustrates the power of prayer by telling the parable of a widow who repeatedly presents her petition to an unrighteous judge. Finally, because of her persistence, the judge grants the widow's petition. At the end of the parable, Jesus explains that we have a righteous Judge who delights to hear our prayers and grant our petitions. As with Hannah, our prayers not only result in the realization of the deepest desires of our heart; they alter the course of history.

Why don't we pray more? Beth Moore has written, "There are parts of our calling, works of the Holy Spirit, and defeats of the darkness that will come no other way than through furious, fervent, faith-filled, unceasing prayer."[2] Being a woman of prayer is one of the most powerful and impactful ways to create a legacy of good for God. We fully expect that when we get to heaven, Jesus will show us how many pitfalls were avoided, how many storms were turned back, how a negative impact was diverted, and how many fortunes were turned to good—all by prayer. When we ponder this truth, the life of one particular praying wife and mother leaps to mind.

The Praying Example of Susanna Wesley

If a passing stranger walking through the rural village of Epworth, England, on any given day between 1700 and 1720 had peered through the window of the home of the rector of the local Anglican church, he might have caught sight of something quite strange. Depending on the time of day, this observer might have seen a woman sitting in a chair with her kitchen apron pulled up over her head while ten children read, studied, or played all around her.

Two of those ten children would have been little boys—John and Charles—who would grow up to shape the course of Christian history and thus change the world. The woman under the apron would have been Susanna Wesley, who assumed this odd posture for two hours almost every day. In a moment you will understand why.

Susanna understood the dynamics of large families. Born the twenty-fifth of twenty-five children in 1669, Susanna Annesley grew up the daughter of a prominent, highly educated minister in cosmopolitan London. She had little formal education, but growing up in an academic household with so many older siblings left her well-read and well-rounded intellectually. She met Samuel Wesley, an aspiring Anglican minister, and married him in 1688, when she was nineteen years old.

Susanna's remaining fifty-three years were far from easy ones. They were characterized by loss, hardship, and struggle. Yet she became a woman of immense legacy, largely through the dual virtues of organization and prayer.

Susanna delivered nineteen children, but nine—including

two sets of twins—died in infancy. Another was accidentally smothered in the night by a nurse as Susanna recovered from labor and delivery.

Her husband, Samuel, did not succeed in his thirty-nine-year assignment as rector of the church at Epworth. An intellectual academic, he simply did not understand or identify with the rural villagers in his parish. Nor did they care for him. When he involved himself from the pulpit in a highly divisive political matter inflaming the entire nation in that era, he earned the hatred of a vast segment of the populace. On two occasions the Wesleys' parsonage burned down, most likely because of arson on the part of Epworth's embittered parishioners. Susanna and the children were seldom spared harassment and insults.

Samuel was not good with money, and he once spent several months in debtors' prison. The parsonage came with a small farm, but Samuel was uninterested in and ill-suited for farm work, so this too was left for Susanna to manage. This was in addition to the huge task of homeschooling all of the children, with their varying ages and gifts.

For decades, Samuel expended all of his energies and most of the family's meager wealth working on an exegetical treatise on the book of Job. The sad irony is that while he was away for long periods of time studying and writing about Job's intense sufferings, his living, breathing wife was enduring real pain and hardship, largely on her own.

Susanna's household organizational skills are the stuff of legend. She knew from personal experience that quality one-on-one time with a parent is hard to come by in a family with many children, yet powerfully important. So she set a rotating schedule through which each of her children spent an hour with her alone before bedtime on a designated night each week.

What is more, she somehow found a way to manage the household and give her large brood of children a world-class education that included both classical and biblical learning. Her girls got the same rigorous education as did her boys, something virtually unheard of in that day. Traditionally, girls of that place and time were taught "feminine" skills such as needlework and music before undertaking the most basic education, such as learning to read. Susanna firmly believed this was wrong-headed. Her girls were taught the same curriculum as her boys. Among the "bylaws" by which she ran her home school was this: "8. That no girl be taught to work till she can read very well; and then that she be kept to her work with the same application, and for the same time, that she was held to in reading. This rule also is much to be observed; for the putting of children to learn sewing before they can read perfectly, is the very reason why so few women can read fit to be heard, and never to be well understood."[3]

School hours were from 9:00 a.m. to noon and then 2:00 p.m. to 5:00 p.m., six days a week. All but the smallest children completed their assigned chores promptly before the start of the school day. As in many one-room schoolhouses in generations past, older children helped teach the younger.

NO EXCUSE FOR NOT PRAYING!

Susanna took her relationship to God as seriously as she did her duties as a wife and mother. Early in her life, she vowed that she would never spend more time in leisure entertainment than she did in prayer and Bible study. Even amid the most complex and busy years of her life as a mother, she still scheduled two hours each day for fellowship with God and time in His Word, and she adhered to that schedule faithfully. The challenge was finding a place of privacy in a house filled to overflowing with children.

Mother Wesley's solution to this was to bring her Bible to her favorite chair and throw her long apron up over her head, forming a sort of tent. This became something akin to the "tent of meeting," the tabernacle in the days of Moses in the Old Testament. Every person in the household, from the smallest toddler to the oldest domestic helpers, knew well to respect this signal. When Susanna was under the apron, she was with God and was not to be disturbed except in the case of the direst emergency. There in the privacy of her little tent, she interceded for her husband and children and plumbed the deep mysteries of God in the Scriptures. This holy discipline equipped her with a thorough and profound knowledge of the Bible.

PRAYER LEADS TO TEACHING

When husband Samuel was away, as was often the case, a substitute minister brought the Sunday morning sermon at the church. Susanna found these messages uninspiring and lacking in spiritual meat. She had a good-sized congregation of her own at home, so she began teaching them the Bible in her kitchen on Sunday afternoons. Soon neighbors began asking if they could attend. Word circulated and others from the area began asking permission to attend as well. So thorough was Susanna's knowledge of the Bible, and so gifted was she at communicating its truths, that on any given Sunday after church, Susanna would have as many as two hundred people in attendance at her informal family Bible study, which started in her home but soon moved to a larger venue.

Susanna passed away in 1742 at the age of seventy-three, living long enough to see her sons John and Charles become world-renowned leaders of the global Christian movement. This is her legacy, forged in large part in those diligent hours of intercession under that makeshift apron tent.

THE LASTING LEGACY OF PRAYER

John Wesley is estimated to have preached to nearly a million people in his long, fruitful life. His powerful, evangelistic services were frequently held in the open air to accommodate audiences in the tens of thousands. Traveling on horseback, he regularly preached three or more times a day, often beginning before daybreak. Even at the age of seventy he preached, without the assistance of modern amplification, to an estimated throng of thirty-two thousand people.

It is hard to overstate John Wesley's theological impact. He remains the dominant theological influence on Methodists and Methodist-heritage groups the world over, including the United Methodist Church, the Methodist Church of Great Britain, and the African Methodist Episcopal Church, all of which played a pivotal role in the abolitionist movement of the nineteenth century.

Wesleyan theology also formed the foundation for the holiness movement in the United States, which includes denominations like the Wesleyan Church, the Free Methodist Church, the Church of the Nazarene, the Christian and Missionary Alliance, the Church of God (Anderson, Indiana), and other groups which compose the colorful mosaic of Pentecostalism and the charismatic movement in North America.

As prolific a writer as he was busy as a preacher, John Wesley has been called the Father of the Religious Paperback. His published sermons, tracts, pamphlets, and booklets number roughly five thousand items. In addition to theology, Wesley wrote about music, marriage, medicine, science, abolitionism, and current events.

Although John married, he and his wife, Mary, had no children. Because of his giving nature toward the poor, the oppressed, and the unevangelized, he left little of material wealth behind when he died in 1791 at the age of eighty-seven. One biographer said John Wesley "was carried to his grave by six poor men 'leaving behind him nothing but a good library of books, a well-worn clergyman's gown . . . and—the Methodist

Church.'"[4] The same writer observed that John's impact was so profound that he in effect "supplied a new starting-point to modern religious history."[5]

John's younger brother Charles was very much a partner in and vital contributor to these accomplishments. A brilliant musician and lyricist, he wrote more than 6,600 hymns, many of which are still in hymnals the world over today.

Charles and his wife, Sarah, had three children who survived infancy, including two boys, Samuel and Charles Jr., who were musical prodigies. Charles Jr. grew up to serve as the personal organist of the English royal family. His brother, Samuel Sebastian Wesley, became one of the most accomplished British composers of the nineteenth century. A contemporary of Mozart, Samuel is sometimes called "The English Mozart."[6]

John and Charles Wesley were passionate lovers of God and powerful persuaders of people. As a result, the brothers were viewed by many of their contemporaries as religious fanatics. History has been far kinder in its verdict. It views them as world changers. And every one of the changes they wrought is part of the legacy of Susanna Wesley. In his 1864 biography, John Kirk wrote of Susanna, "Her name has been everywhere received with respect; and by a large and influential Christian Community it has been cherished with strongest affection. Her success in the education of her children has been the theme of universal admiration; and no one has yet ventured to hazard even a conjecture as to how much the cause of religion and the well-being of the human race are indebted to her steady piety and extraordinary talents."[7]

We hope that as you read these stories of Hannah and Susanna Wesley, you'll grab on to the power of them. Hannah's prayer life was incredibly intertwined with her faith and knowledge of God's Word. She didn't always need to say her prayers out loud. They were part of the fabric of her life.

And for Susanna Wesley, there was no amount of distraction that could keep her from prayer and the Bible. That kind of life, deeply rooted, produced great fruit, as evidenced not only by the people who came to hear her teach but also by the children she influenced. The great truth in her story is how prayer does not occupy the stage of activity. Its power is in the quiet trust of gentle souls who are willing to pull away from the everyday to commune with God.

In our own lifetimes, we have personally witnessed what a praying matriarch of a Christian family can accomplish. My (Jackie's) great-grandmother, grandmother, and mother were all tremendously influential in my life. As a result of their prayers for me, and because I witnessed their communication with God, the most impactful, life-changing moment in my life began with a prayer of my own when I was a young girl. I greatly value my opportunity to communicate with God—anywhere, anytime— knowing that He always hears and I can hand over my fears, anxiety, stress, health, insufficiencies, emotions, you name it. God can handle it. More important, He helps me handle things much better and be a better me.

My mother, Nita, has always been a woman of prayer. She takes seriously the call of a mother to pray over her children and grandchildren. It isn't unusual to hear her giving a scripturally sound mini sermon to her grandchildren when she is around them. And her grandmother, Fannie, and her mother, Delia, were also women who often exercised their privilege to pray. This has been passed down to me.

These days, it isn't unusual for me to wake up during the night, feeling a nudge in my spirit to pray for certain people. I count it a privilege to have the Spirit of God bring people to my mind so I can present their names and needs before the throne of heaven. I am thankful to have witnessed the power of prayer throughout my childhood at my grandmother's side and my mother's side. I can identify with Susanna Wesley, as a mother of a large family. I find that the plans I have for each day can quickly change with my family's needs. The best way for me to start my day is with a prayer before I even get out of bed. It doesn't have to be long, but inviting God to be a part of my daily walk always gets me started in the right direction. I'm just so thankful that God hears our intimate communication with Him anywhere and anytime. My practice of prayer today is part of my daily devotionals and of late-night vigils when my children are in their beds—although I can promise you, my prayer life is still a work in progress!

With both a mother and a mother-in-law committed to prayer over the many needs we have had as a family, I have no doubt that God has heard my name brought before Him many times. What an amazing legacy. What a responsibility I feel to carry it on and pass it forward.

Another matriarch of our family is Barbara Green—our mother-in-law and grandmother respectively—who is a woman very devoted to prayer.

The Prayers of Barbara Green

People who have a deep heart for prayer seem to quietly go about using their gift. They may even downplay it.

Such is the case with Barbara Green. My (Jackie's) husband, Steve, and his siblings all have their favorite stories of instances when, in difficult times, their mother pointed them to prayer rather than worry. She not only preached this; she modeled it. She prayed each of her children into the kingdom of God through a genuine, personal relationship with Jesus Christ. She prayed them through the sometimes-perilous teen years. She also prayed the whole family through the risk-filled, arduous years of launching Hobby Lobby from the family's garage.

She doesn't talk much about herself or her devotional life, but on numerous occasions I've heard my father-in-law, David, say things like, "Well, Barbara was up in the middle of the night praying again last night." If he didn't mention it, no one but God would ever know. Nevertheless, to observe her life is to see that she wholeheartedly believes and exemplifies something Corrie ten Boom once said: "Any concern too small to be turned into a prayer is too small to be made into a burden."[8] Barbara was and continues to be a woman whose significant and growing legacy is in large part built on the power of prayer. Barbara tells me that she asks the Lord to nudge her awake in the middle of the night to pray. As part of her discipline, she'll wake up, cover herself with what she calls her prayer shawl, and begin to pray as God leads her for people and for the issues of the day. She'll record her insights and interactions in her journal, and by now of course she has dozens and dozens of these diaries of prayer.

This lifestyle of prayer, as well as her love for the Word of God, certainly made a deep and powerful impression on her grandchildren. I recently came across an email I sent to Barbara and my mother many years ago, back when Lauren was only sixteen. In it, I told Lauren's grandmothers that I just wanted to share some of the pride and gratitude I was feeling after learning that Lauren, on her own and without prompting from us, had just finished reading the Bible from beginning to end. I wanted them to know that the spiritual example they had provided to their grandchildren was bearing fruit in an emerging legacy of faith.

MY GRANDMOTHER'S PRAYER LEGACY

There's little doubt that my grandmother has had a big impact on me (Lauren). The inspiration to read the whole Bible in a year came when, as an eighth-grader, I attended the funeral of a gifted young Christian athlete at a local high school. He had a younger sister in our church youth group who was my age. At his service, I heard some of his teammates and classmates talk about how Justin was always reading his Bible and journaling. They talked about how his Christian witness and clear love for the Word of God challenged and inspired them. Hearing about this young man and his impact on others, at such a young age, made a powerful impression on me.

Up to that point, I think I had sort of viewed Bible study as something adults did. I certainly grew up seeing my parents reading their Bibles and freely quoting Scripture. Every important adult I loved and admired was a Bible reader. So I grew up thinking, *Sure, someday when I'm an adult, I'll do that too.* But hearing about how Justin had already begun to make the Bible a key part of his life made me realize, *I can start now.* You're never too young to start reading the Bible.

It took me a while to find the resolve to get started, but at some point during my tenth-grade year, I got a Bible that had a "Read the Bible Through in a Year" reading plan and got going. I enjoyed the sense of achievement and progress that came from checking off the box beside each day's reading each night before bed. A little more than a year later, I reached the final chapter of Revelation and checked off that last box.

I honestly don't recall going into my parents' bedroom that night to share my accomplishment, but my mother remembers it vividly. That's when she sent that email to my grandmothers.

Not long afterward, my grandmother Barbara brought me a keepsake gift to mark the accomplishment. It was a prayer shawl very much like one she was given when she was young. Such shawls were popular in certain Christian faith traditions in previous generations. The idea was to attach to the fabric of the wrap meaningful pins that served as reminders to pray for certain people or things. One pin might serve as a reminder to pray for your parents. Another, a reminder to pray for a certain missionary, nation, or cause. The prayer shawl of a longtime, committed intercessor might be covered with such prompts.

I'm not sure I fully appreciated how special and meaningful that gift was back when I was sixteen, but I do now. And more than anything else, it challenges me to be the kind of prayer warrior my grandmothers have both been for all of us through the years.

PRAYER IN THE STORM

Barbara's consistent, faith-filled, Word-based intercession has been an anchor in the storms for both our family and the family business through the years. We've had some challenging times as a company and a family, and yet prayer has always been a constant.

Nevertheless, 2012 brought both our business and our family the severest test we had ever faced. That year started a multiyear crisis that tested to the core our commitments to our biblical convictions, threatened to bring an abrupt end to the enterprise that so many had worked so hard to build through the years, and took us all to the steps of the US Supreme Court.

As we pointed out in the opening of this book, the Green family has always sought to honor God by operating Hobby Lobby in accordance with biblical principles. That is why, contrary to all industry standards and the practices of our competitors, all of the company's stores are closed on Sundays and operate only sixty-six hours per week. This allows our employees to spend evenings and Sundays with their families. Our company also starts all full-time hourly workers at more than double the federal minimum wage, because we believe in treating people well.

Under provisions of the Affordable Care Act—which passed and was signed into law in 2010 and phased into effect over the next few years—businesses above a certain size in the United States were required to provide insurance that covered twenty different forms of contraception. Among these twenty contraception methods were four that were potentially life-terminating drugs and devices. The Federal Department of Health and Human Services began enforcing this mandate in 2012. Businesses that failed to comply with these requirements faced potentially millions of dollars in fines to the IRS.

This requirement created a moral dilemma for us at Hobby Lobby, and for hundreds, perhaps thousands, of other closely held companies owned by people of faith with pro-life convictions. We were faced with either violating a portion of the law or violating our Christian conscience. As the implications of the law became fully visible to David Green and the rest of the family in the company's leadership, that moral dilemma became painfully obvious.

As we studied the requirements of the law, it became clear that we had no moral objection to sixteen of the twenty contraceptives required in the mandate. The excellent health insurance provided to full-time Hobby Lobby employees had contained coverage for those unobjectionable, non–life-ending drugs and devices for quite some time. However, the more we studied the facts of the medical science behind those other four methods, including drugs like the morning-after pill and the week-after pill, the clearer it became that our faith-informed convictions about the sanctity of human life would not allow us to fund their coverage.

For us not to provide those products freely is not forcing our convictions on any other person or family. It would go against our faith, which comes from the Bible, to force our convictions on another individual. For our part, we knew in our hearts that we were going to have to take a stand. We also knew that such a stand might mean the crippling or even dismantling of the business that David and Barbara Green, along with their three adult children and other family members, had poured their lives and hearts into for more than four decades. We also felt the weight of responsibility to the more than thirty-five thousand employees we'd always tried to do right by.

PRAYING AS A FAMILY

Fighting these conscience-violating aspects of the Affordable Care Act in the legal system wasn't a comfortable scenario for us. We were raised not to be litigious. But in the end, we felt we had one choice: to stand up for our convictions and take the issue to court. We were on the clock, so to speak. In a few short months, the problematic provisions would be kicking in. If we didn't come into full compliance, we faced the prospect of incurring fines that could have amounted to $1.3 million— per day! What is more, we knew there were thousands of other Christian-owned businesses and charities facing the same crisis of conscience. Though many businesses stepped up to defend their religious freedom, our suit (which the courts combined with that of a Pennsylvania cabinet-making company) ended up being at the front of the line. Speaking of charities, ultimately our suit ran parallel with that of another challenge to the law being brought by the Catholic charity Little Sisters of the Poor.

Still, it was a huge decision for our family, with enormous implications. So three generations of Greens gathered in a living room to pray, count the cost, and decide what to do. In the end, we were all in agreement. We had to put a stake in the ground. Our consciences would not permit us to do anything else, regardless of the cost or risks.

What followed was nearly two years of battles in the court system. Initially, a lower court ruled against us, so we appealed to the next level. When that federal court also ruled against us, we appealed again. In the end, we found our case being appealed to the United States Supreme Court. That was possible, however, only if they agreed to hear the case. Because of conflicting rulings in the lower courts, they did.

Throughout that two-year period, life went on. There was a nationwide business to run and the huge Museum of the Bible project to plan. This whole contraception issue had arisen right after we stepped out to purchase the land for the building in Washington, D.C. It's almost as if, at a spiritual level, we took the biggest step of faith of our lives and were immediately faced with the biggest challenge in our family's history. Throughout that period, wherever we went in the country, people approached us to let us know they were praying for us, some even saying they prayed for our family every day. Everywhere we went, strangers would walk up to us and thank us for standing up for justice, for freedom of religion. Those many, many prayers made a difference. It was a humbling thing.

Of course, it wasn't just others doing all the praying. Because we knew we were just one company taking on the United States government, we all prayed constantly. It was a great comfort to know that Barbara was also up most nights praying, taking our needs to God.

Each defeat in the lower courts was discouraging and troubling, but with each setback, Barbara would say, "God has this. The battle belongs to the Lord." We would then all regather our resolve and press on to the next step.

In any event, on March 25, 2014, oral arguments at the historic US Supreme Court building in Washington began. David and Barbara Green, along with their three adult children and their spouses (including me, Jackie), a nephew and his spouse, and one granddaughter (me, Lauren), were there to watch the arguments commence. It was a surreal experience to walk up those marble steps, through those doors, and into the marble halls of the building that has witnessed so much history.

Speaking of those steps, the next day many of the major newspapers in the nation carried a front-page photo of our family group walking down those steps at the end of the day. It was beginning to snow, and the marble was growing slippery. There we are, a cluster of people, holding on to each other for support as we navigate those steps, with dozens of television cameras pointed at us. Front and center of our squad in the photo is Barbara, beaming at the throng of cheering, sign-holding well-wishers gathered outside the building.

Today an enlarged version of that photo hangs on the wall in the conference room of our Family Legacy Center in Oklahoma City as a reminder that prayer, faith, and family unity can carry us through any adversity and create a positive legacy, not just for our family but also for families of faith and conscience all over the nation.

Three months later—on June 30, 2014—most of those same people, plus many others who couldn't make the trip to Washington, gathered to watch a live feed of the announcement of the Supreme Court ruling. When the historic ruling came down, we (and our husbands) were overseas on Museum of the Bible business. So at the climactic moment, we were huddled around an iPad in a conference room in Oxford, England, joining the family group at the Hobby Lobby headquarters in Oklahoma City via Skype. We couldn't be there physically, but we still wanted to feel like we were all together when we heard the news—good or bad.

In the moments before the ruling, we were breathless yet confident in God's prevailing grace. When it was announced that the US Supreme Court had ruled 5–4 in our favor, celebration erupted simultaneously in Oklahoma City and in Oxford. The next day's *New York Times* headline read, "Supreme Court Rejects Contraceptives Mandate for Some Corporations: Justices Rule in Favor of Hobby Lobby."[9]

Of course, we were relieved beyond belief, but not surprised. At the deepest levels of our souls, we had always carried an assurance that everything was going to be all right. We believed that Barbara's prayers, our prayers, and the prayers of thousands and thousands of fellow believers across the country and around the world had gone ahead of us to make a way.

THE PRAYER COVERING

We will never forget the outpouring of support we experienced as we walked through that crazy, two-year season of spiritual warfare. The expressions of solidarity and gratitude we heard everywhere we went were a tremendous source of encouragement and strength.

Of course, I (Jackie) had to learn how to encourage myself as well. Because of the issues at the heart of our case, as well as the polarized, ugly nature of our politics these days, we knew that our entire family and business were under tremendous scrutiny. I have to admit I battled fear and frustration.

The whole situation carried my natural tendency to be a "worry wart," as my mother would say, to a whole new level. I had to start each day with prayer as soon as my eyes opened. If I didn't, fearful thoughts would come in like a flood and try to overwhelm me. I would pray until the peace of God began to flow over me. Only then would I get up and begin my day.

At the same time, the constant flow of encouragement and support from around the country was amazing. We heard these messages countless times and never got tired of it. On the contrary, they were life to us. I remember Steve and I talking about how the support we experienced reminded us of the biblical account of Aaron and Hur holding up the arms of Moses while the Israelites were in a battle. Without a doubt, we had a whole army of the Lord behind us in our fight, praying and interceding. We know that God hears the prayers of His people. We just happened to be the ones on the front line. Of course, we didn't want to be there. No sane person does. Still, there we were, and we were not alone. Truly, God gave me a peace that surpasses understanding in the midst of a two-year storm.

We have discovered that when we press into God—through prayer, meditating on Scriptures, and sometimes seeking wise counsel from others who are strong in their faith—we find strength. It isn't always instantaneous, however. Living this way requires patience. Yet when we truly believe that God loves us, that He is all-powerful, all-knowing, and ever-present, and that we can trust Him to be with us through even the fiercest trials, strength comes. We can face the unknown. We can be assured that we will get through it, because we know who goes before us. We know who stands behind us. We know who walks beside us.

From Hannah, to Susanna Wesley, to Barbara Green, to a praying family, to the prayer covering provided by the body of believers, we learn that while prayer is not necessarily the most visible activity, it is the most powerful. Prayer provides protection and strength. Prayer is not for the casual participant. It takes work. It forces us to dig in deep—sometimes in anguish, and sometimes in the early morning hours. It is a lifestyle that is sacred and bears sacred fruit. It provides light in the storms. And if we have only one life, how much better if our path is lighted by prayer.

CHAPTER 12

THE LEGACY OF LOYALTY

*Courage and kindness, loyalty and truth are
always the same and are always needed.*

—Laura Ingalls Wilder[1]

We sometimes wonder why people stick with a person or a cause even when it seems like they should give up. Loyalty is hard to define but unmistakable when in action. And it seems that it is an ancient valued trait, because we see this in Scripture: "Never let go of loyalty and faithfulness. Tie them around your neck; write them on your heart. If you do this, both God and people will be pleased with you" (Prov. 3:3–4 GNT). Faith looks to the future with confidence in what can't be seen. Loyalty puts feet to that faith. When we see through the eyes of faith, we know that staying true to a cause or person will be worth it in the long term, no matter what it may cost us today.

The Time-Honored Story of Loyalty

Years ago, hard times drove Naomi and her husband out of Judah to the land of the Moabites. Now a wave of even greater calamity is forcing her back home to the land of her people. Widowed and frail, she is not sure whether she will survive the journey or how she will live if she manages to get there.

Hunger has a way of compelling hard choices. Naomi and

her husband, Elimelech, were third-generation Israelites in the land of promise. Their grandparents—members of the tribe of Judah—had been a part of the conquest of Canaan under Joshua and had settled near the village that would one day be called Bethlehem.

The couple had two small sons and a good life. Then a severe famine wiped out both their livelihood and any hope of recovery. Travelers brought reports that things were much better back on the other side of the Jordan River. So Elimelech made the hard choice of uprooting his young family and heading for what was essentially hostile territory. They gathered what personal belongings they could carry and retraced the path their Israelite forefathers had walked with such hope less than a century earlier. They crossed the Jordan River from west to east. And they began to scratch out a life as strangers in a new land.

It had been difficult, but they survived. The boys grew up and married local Moabite girls. This was initially a bitter pill for Naomi and Elimelech to swallow. After all, the Moabites were a related race of people descended from the incestuous union of Lot and his two daughters in the aftermath of the divine destruction of Sodom and Gomorrah. Still, Naomi grew to love Orpah and Ruth, her new daughters-in-law. But just when life was beginning to brighten, with the prospect of grandchildren on the horizon, tragedy struck. In a short space of time, all three men—Naomi's husband and her two sons—died. Three widows now stood destitute.

THE CHOICE OF LOYALTY

Heartbroken and frightened, Naomi sees no choice but to return to Bethlehem and hope for benevolence from her own people. This is certainly more realistic than expecting kindness from these strange Moabites, who never completely accepted her and her late husband.

Of course, the two daughters-in-law of whom she has grown so fond would feel equally out of place back in Judah. Besides, they still have family in Moab. Even though she is quite dependent on their strength and help, she selflessly releases them from the bonds forged by their marriages to her sons. She insists that they return to their mothers' households, where their prospects for remarrying and having children are far greater.

After a little coaxing, Orpah agrees and departs for her family's village. Ruth is not so easily dismissed. She clearly views her covenantal vows with profound seriousness. The more intently Naomi insists that Ruth, for her own good, abandon Naomi to her fate, the more passionately does the young Moabitess refuse.

Ruth makes her closing case to Naomi in what will become one of the most poignant and powerful professions of loyalty ever recorded in sacred literature.

> "Entreat me not to leave you,
> Or to turn back from following after you;
> For wherever you go, I will go;
> And wherever you lodge, I will lodge;
> Your people shall be my people,
> And your God, my God.
> Where you die, I will die,
> And there will I be buried.
> The LORD do so to me, and more also,
> If anything but death parts you and me."
>
> —Ruth 1:16–17 NKJV

Nothing about Ruth's decision makes sense. Her mother-in-law is not a blood relative. Ruth cannot imagine that Naomi will provide a living or a husband for her. She will be a stranger in a strange land. Yet there is something about Naomi's faith that strikes a chord in Ruth's soul. And even though Ruth cannot know the future, she decides to follow Naomi. Unconditionally. For the rest of her days. Loyalty.

She embraces the covenant people to whom Naomi belongs and the faith that Naomi holds dear. Ruth will accompany Naomi back to Judah and eventually be married to a kind and noble man of Israel. Together Ruth and Boaz will produce a son who will become a direct ancestor of King David, and ultimately of the King of Kings.

That's quite a legacy for a Moabite woman of obscure lineage. Furthermore, her example of fierce, selfless loyalty will shine through the millennia and inspire countless others.

WHERE DOES LOYALTY STAND?

We live in an age in which *self*-interest is the dominant ethic of the culture. Many people appear to have taken Shakespeare's famous advice in *Hamlet* to heart: "Above all, to thine own self be true." Of course, being first, last, and always true to self frequently requires being untrue to others. As a result, today's promises, oaths, and even vows—including the most sacred of these, marriage vows—are cast aside the moment they become inconvenient. Loyalty has fallen out of fashion.

Even postmodern thinkers such as the *Wall Street Journal*'s Eric Felten have recognized that our culture has lost something important and precious in our age of flimsy connections and even flimsier promises: "Our modern, rootless times do seem to be a particularly inhospitable environment for loyalty. We come and go so relentlessly that our friendships can't but come and go too. What sort of loyalty is there in the age of Facebook, when friendship is a costless transaction, a business of flip reciprocity. . . . Friendship held together by nothing more permanent than hyperlinks is hardly the stuff of selfless fidelity."[2]

Yet in God's social economy, loyalty remains a powerful legacy-building force. This shouldn't surprise us. All of God's actions and interactions with us, His creatures, have been built on covenant. And a covenant is nothing more than a solemn, sacred agreement between parties to be true to one another. This is why God is so frequently described in His Word as being faithful. This speaks to His fidelity to His covenant promises: "Know therefore that the LORD your God is God; he is the faithful God, keeping his covenant of love to a thousand generations of those who love him and keep his commandments" (Deut. 7:9).

Marriage too is a form of covenant that stands or falls on the strength of the loyalty of husband and wife to one another. Likewise, friendships, as well as the covenantal bonds that connect believers engaged in the work of God's kingdom together, depend on loyalty and fidelity. As Jesus declared to His disciples, "There is no greater love than to lay down one's life for one's friends" (John 15:13 NLT).

Loyalty to the Mission

When we think about this kind of loyalty—to God, to co-laborers, and to a shared sense of sacred mission—our minds immediately turn to the famous account of Jim Elliot and four fellow missionaries killed in 1956 by the reclusive Huaorani tribe in Ecuador as the men attempted to make first contact in the hope of bringing them the gospel.

The subsequent book by Elliot's wife, Elisabeth, *Through Gates of Splendor*, became an international bestseller in the late 1950s.

In 2002, Mart Green, my (Jackie's) brother-in-law, oversaw production of a powerful documentary that explored these amazing events. Titled *Beyond the Gates of Splendor*, the moving film won the Crystal Heart Award at the Heartland Film Festival and the Audience Favorite Documentary Award at the

Palm Beach Film Festival shortly after its release. Then in 2006, Mart's company released *The End of the Spear*, a feature-length film dramatization of this story. The launch of the film was timed to coincide with the fiftieth anniversary of the deaths of the Ecuadoran missionaries. *The End of the Spear* introduced a new generation to this remarkable story of forgiveness, loyalty, and breakthrough.

In 2001, I (Lauren) had the opportunity to travel with my father, siblings, and other family members down to Ecuador and spend time in the jungle with the very people of the Huaorani tribe who killed the five missionaries. Experiencing life with the Huaorani for nearly a week, I saw the legacy of Elisabeth Elliot and Rachel Saint's impact lived out in the people's daily life.

We spent time with the Huaorani and got to know their culture. They had been one of the most violent people groups in the world at one time, just decades earlier. Now they were a kind, peaceful people. It was a stark contrast to what I had read about their previous way of life, which included high numbers of homicides.

I remember one day, we were doing a bit of target practice with the wooden spears that the Huaorani used to hunt. They were going to be hunting for dinner later that day, so they set up a tree stump as the target, and we all took turns trying to hit the target with the spear. We were all terrible, while the Huaorani were quite skilled! This was their way of providing food for their families, so they had to be.

Looking back, I realize that there wasn't one moment when I was afraid they might turn those spears on me or the rest of our family. We had lived with these people, seen their love for us and for each other. And while just a few decades before, no one could have imagined getting near their tribe without being speared to death, just like the five missionaries, it was different now. The gospel of Jesus Christ as revealed in Scripture had found its way into the lives of this people group, and they were forever—radically—changed. The faithful work of Elisabeth and Rachel had transformed one of the most violent tribes in the world to a peaceful, Bible-believing people.

THE LOYALTY STORY MANY DON'T KNOW

Many Christians are familiar with the story of how Elisabeth Elliot continued her efforts to evangelize the very tribe that killed her husband. She spent two years as a missionary to the Huaorani and witnessed a breakthrough that resulted in the salvation of the tribal leaders who had carried out the deadly attack on the five missionaries. Far fewer people have heard of the work of another woman who lost a loved one to a Huaorani spear on the Amazonian riverbank that day. And few have heard that this woman is a big part of the reason the gospel took root among these warrior people.

When Elisabeth Elliot flew back into the same remote jungle territory in which her husband had been murdered, Rachel Saint was at her side.

Years before the murders occurred, Rachel, a gifted linguist, had worked for Wycliffe Bible Translators in Peru for several years, translating the Bible into the languages of two indigenous tribes. While there, she heard reports of a mysterious, feared warrior tribe in neighboring Ecuador. The Huaorani were known to be one of the last unreached people groups in the Western Hemisphere—unreached because of their extreme isolation in the depths of the Amazon rain forest and because of their ruthless, xenophobic territorialism. The group had been engaged in deadly disputes with neighboring Amazon tribes as long as anyone could remember. These resulted in ongoing and escalating tit-for-tat killings and reprisals between the groups.

Rachel felt powerfully drawn to the challenge of bringing the good news to this uncharted frontier for evangelism. So in

February 1955, she and a friend moved to an Ecuadoran mission station near Huaorani territory, where Rachel's younger brother, Nate, was working as a bush pilot. There Rachel dove headlong into learning the Huaorani language with the help of an exiled Huaorani woman named Dayuma.

Shortly thereafter, her brother Nate, Jim Elliot, and three other men began making plans to make contact with the Huaorani. This included making numerous flights over the main Huaorani village, lowering gifts by rope and bucket. After a few such trips, the missionaries were encouraged to find the tribesmen reciprocating by placing gifts of their own in the bucket. Finally, in January of 1956, the group felt it was time to take the huge step of making personal contact.

You already know that the effort ended in heartache. When the men failed to check in at the appointed time with their wives, who were in charge of monitoring the radio, an armed search party was sent after them. Five spear-pierced bodies were found near the riverbank beach on which they'd come ashore. Nate Saint, Jim Elliot, and the others were buried there near the spot where they had lost their lives for the sake of the gospel. News of the massacre made headlines the world over.

Rachel's and Elisabeth's responses to the death of their loved ones further stunned a watching world. These profoundly spiritual, Word-grounded women did not fall apart. Nor did they succumb to anger, bitterness, or resentment. The word that best characterizes the actions of Rachel Saint and the others in the weeks, months, and years that followed is *loyalty*—to God, to the mission that the men gave their lives trying to advance, and, most remarkably, to the Huaorani.

Yes, Rachel's and the other women's first impulse was to express trust and confidence in their heavenly Father. In the wake of the tragedy, they ran *to* Him rather than from Him, affirming His goodness and love.

LOYALTY THAT DOESN'T MAKE SENSE

At the same time, both Rachel Saint and Elisabeth Elliot clearly believed—and demonstrated by their actions—that the only way to be faithful to the sense of calling they shared with their fallen loved ones was to pick up where they had left off. If Nate Saint, Jim Elliot, and the others believed that reaching the Huaorani with the message of Christ was worth risking all, that was surely still true after their deaths.

In the months after the tragedy, Rachel told friends and relatives that she believed Nate's death at the hands of those tribesmen bonded her to them in a powerful way. After all, if she turned away from the quest to evangelize the Huaorani now, Nate's death would have been in vain. Thus her sense of fidelity extended even to the individuals who killed her brother. Especially so.

A little more than two and a half years after her brother's body was discovered on that jungle riverbank, Rachel Saint was headed into Huaorani territory with Elisabeth Elliot and their first convert, Dayuma. They were received by the tribe because, as women, they were not perceived as a threat. Soon the gospel was taking root in the hearts of the people there, including the very men who killed the five missionaries.

Elisabeth Elliot stayed two years before returning to the United States to write and speak. Rachel Saint never left the Huaorani. She remained with the Huaorani people in the jungle, teaching, discipling, and translating books of the Bible into the local language, until she died at the age of eighty, known to the tribe as "Star." She is buried there, in a hallowed plot of ground near where her brother's body was laid so many decades ago.

This story of redemption, restoration, and rebirth through loyalty has a particularly poignant chapter. Rachel's martyred brother Nate had two small children, Steve and Kathy. When they were old enough, they visited their aunt deep in the jungle.

There, for the first time, they saw the place where the father they could hardly remember had died for the cause of Christ.[3]

While on that visit, they mentioned that they had never been baptized. So on a Sunday morning, there at the river where their father was killed, they were baptized by the pastor and head of the Huaorani tribe, Kimo, the leader of the group who had killed their father and the other missionaries years before. Remarkably, today the children and grandchildren of Steve lovingly refer to the man who killed Nate Saint as their grandfather. This is the power of loyalty.

Rachel Saint's legacy is not only a growing community of second- and third-generation believers who can read the Bible in their native tongue in the heart of the Ecuadoran jungle, as remarkable as that might be. It extends to the untold thousands who have taken inspiration from the examples of the courageous women who rejected retribution or bitterness, choosing mercy and evangelistic compassion instead.

Biblical loyalty is a product of love. It manifests in a variety of ways among God's people. We see it on display in simple yet profound forms all around us. It is there in the relentless prayers of a heartbroken parent for a wayward, rebellious child. It is there when expectant parents receive unwelcome news from the obstetrician and choose life anyway. We see it when disease or an accident dramatically changes the needs of a loved one.

Nowhere is love's loyalty more necessary or more beautiful than when a person is called on to walk through the agonizing decline of dementia with someone they love. As life spans have increased in the Western world, cases of Alzheimer's disease and other forms of dementia have soared. As a result, tens of thousands of believers today find themselves slowly losing the spouse they love and to whom they pledged before God to "love, cherish, and care for" until death parts them.

As we said earlier, loyalty flows out of love in one form or another. So it isn't wholly surprising when a person demonstrates sacrificial loyalty toward a spouse, a child, or a parent. In a sense, this loyalty flows naturally, and therefore, to a certain extent, it is expected in our culture. Yet there are degrees of loyalty, and because Christians are called to be faithful, loving, patient, kind, good, and gentle, they are often willing to be self-sacrificing and long-suffering. How could the followers of Jesus Christ, the self-sacrificial Lamb of God, be otherwise? The One we serve and who lives within us exemplified selflessness at every turn. He is the One whose name is revealed, in the book of Revelation, to be "Faithful and True" (Rev. 19:11).

It is no coincidence that the bonds of family loyalty in our nation are dissolving in parallel with our culture's rejection of Christianity and biblical values. Fidelity between husbands and wives, the willingness of men to take responsibility for the children they father, and the assumption that adult children will care for aging parents are all in freefall. Yes, the virtue of sacrificial loyalty is becoming less and less of a given, even among believers. This makes the virtue of loyalty more precious in our day.

Of course, loyalty is even more remarkable and powerful when we see it displayed outside the borders of family ties. Rachel Saint and Elisabeth Elliot were not just loyal to their martyred loved ones. Their actions were driven by loyalty to the *cause* in which they all passionately believed and for which their dear ones sacrificed their lives. Loyalty can also be extended to a friend, to a local church, to an institution, or to a neighborhood or community.

The Power of Loyalty

It's fitting to close this book with one of the great stories of loyalty of our time.

Ruth Bell was born in the province of Jiangsu, China, in 1920, the daughter of Presbyterian medical missionaries there—the second-oldest child of Dr. Nelson and Virginia Bell. At the volatile, pivotal age of thirteen, Ruth was sent to a boarding school in Pyongyang, Korea, now the capital of North Korea. In 1933, the Korean peninsula was unified but under occupation by the Japanese Empire. In these formative years, this missionary kid wholly surrendered to Christ and developed a passionate, authentic faith of her own—one that would sustain her all her life.

When she was sixteen, her parents' missionary furlough gave her the opportunity to finish high school in the United States. A small town in the mountains of western North Carolina, at the height of the Great Depression, became Ruth's first extended taste of American life. From there, she entered Wheaton College in Illinois with a powerful conviction that she was called to follow in her parents' footsteps and become a missionary in the Far East. She specifically had a heart for the remote and largely unreached nation of Tibet.

Her sense of calling underwent a transformative crisis when she met and fell in love with a fellow student there at Wheaton, a young man who also sensed a burning, undeniable ministry call on his life. This young man had preaching, not foreign missions, in his heart. His name was William, but everyone called him Billy. Billy Graham.

For a time, Ruth felt that Billy could not possibly be God's man for her, despite the genuine love she felt in her heart for him. After all, she had a call to world missions. Her sights were resolutely set on Tibet. And for all she knew, this boy and his future helpmeet were headed for a meaningful but quiet life of pastoring small churches in rural corners of his native North Carolina. Would she give up her dream of missions for this man?

Ruth ultimately set aside her fears and confusion and gave her hand and heart to Billy, trusting God to sort out any seeming conflicts in their callings. As a young woman who placed the highest value on the Word of God, she came to recognize that she was not only called to follow her husband as he led their family; her primary mission was to support and help him succeed in *his* calling. She could not possibly have dreamed that he would one day be the premier soul-winning evangelist of the twentieth century, used to bring millions to Christ, not only in the United States but throughout the world.

LOYALTY IN THE EVERYDAY

Ruth loyally and faithfully worked alongside her soulmate for the next forty-three years, right up to the day of her home-going in 2007. In her child-rearing years, this often meant staying at home and caring for their five children as Billy traveled the world, preaching to stadiums full of people. It meant praying for her husband and helping him stay grounded as he navigated the treacherous waters of becoming the first celebrity preacher of the television age.

Ruth also exhibited a fierce loyalty to her children as several of them—coming of age in the turbulent, revolutionary 1960s—spent seasons of time seeming to walk away from the faith of their parents or pursue self-destructive lifestyles. Years later she would write with transparency and grace of these struggles, in order to encourage other Christian parents facing the same circumstances. In the introduction to *Prodigals and Those Who Love Them*, Ruth wrote, "For some reason they are usually thought of as teenage boys. But prodigals are not limited in gender, race, age, or color. They do have one thing in common: They have left home . . . and they are missed. For any who might be waiting the return of a loved prodigal, I venture to share some of the comfort and assurance I gathered from a variety of sources during the years of our waiting."[4]

What a beautiful and poignant way to describe the vigil of prayer every Christian parent of a wayward child knows so well. That vigil in the night watch is a pure expression of loyal love.

In the previous chapter, I (Jackie) shared some details of

the fears and worries I battled as we walked through that high-stakes, high-profile Supreme Court adventure. I shared how it seemed that it was in the dark of the night that my mind was most vulnerable. It's comforting to know that a woman like Ruth Bell Graham fought similar battles. She once wrote, "When it is dark and the imagination runs wild, there are fears that only a mother can understand. Suddenly the Lord said to me, 'Quit studying the problems and start studying the promises.'"[5]

How right and appropriate that when faced with our fears, we turn to God's Word and prayer. The night God challenged Ruth to turn to the Word, Ruth opened up her Bible and read Philippians 4:6: "Do not be anxious about anything, but in every situation, by prayer and petition, with thanksgiving, present your requests to God." For Ruth, that verse marked a new beginning. "So I put down my Bible and spent time worshiping Him for who He is and what He is. . . . And you know what happened? It was as if someone suddenly turned on the lights in my mind and heart, and the little fears and worries which, like mice and cockroaches, had been nibbling away in the darkness, suddenly scuttled for cover. That was when I learned that worship and worry cannot live in the same heart."[6]

I love the way Ruth pointed us to the Word of God as our refuge in the day of trouble. That has been my experience as well. The promises and precepts of God are an unshakeable refuge in the inevitable storms of life.

LOYALTY TO THE BIBLE

Ruth Bell Graham's faithfulness to the Scriptures never faltered throughout her long, fruitful life. The consistent testimony of people who knew her best was that the Bible was life to her. Just how much she treasured the Word of God is illustrated by an anecdote from her last few years of life—a season sadly marred by frailty, failing health, and deteriorating vision.

One day a grandson from Florida came to the mountaintop cabin that had been the Grahams' home since the 1940s. Ruth was largely confined to her bed at the time. Upon entering the long-familiar room, he was surprised to see a new feature. The entire circumference of the room had two rows of new shelves on the walls. And on those shelves were more large three-ring binders than he'd ever seen in one place other than an office supply store. Every shelf on every wall was filled. Puzzled, he asked his grandmother what was going on.

She explained that her eyesight had become so poor that the text of even the giant-print versions of the Bible had become far too small for her to read. Yet not being able to read the Bible for herself was more than she could bear. So a team of faithful helpers had printed out the text of the entire Bible in enormous type and collected them in those binders, each of the Bible's sixty-six books requiring numerous volumes.

She was delighted to once again be able to read those great and precious promises. This remarkable woman exemplified loyalty in every area of her life. Yet at the end of her well-run race, it was loyalty to the Word of God that defined her and her legacy.

Loyalty. Ruth the Moabitess. Elisabeth Elliot. Rachel Saint. Ruth Bell Graham. Throughout this book, we've sought to emphasize that the names on the page are not to be idolized. They are women like us—imperfect people who find themselves in complex times and choose to actively seek God as they take their next step. Ruth the Moabitess was a widow, a foreigner who followed her mother-in-law. Elisabeth Elliot and Rachel Saint believed that their God was bigger than death and that the mission was bigger than their own safety. Ruth Bell Graham was willing to forego her dream in order to be part of her husband's dream. Each left a profound legacy, and within their stories, perhaps we can see our stories: the stories of everyday women who faithfully follow Christ, and in doing so, build a lasting legacy.

STEWARDING YOUR "ONLY ONE LIFE"

*Lord, remind me how brief my time on
earth will be. Remind me that my days are
numbered—how fleeting my life is.*

—Psalm 39:4 NLT

nly one life.

The divine gift of a single, fragile life span is all any
of us have been granted. Rich and poor, great and small,
woman and man, it doesn't matter. One is all we get. Which
makes the signature wisdom of Marie Green's favorite quote,
with which we began this journey, so very important: "Only one
life, 'twill soon be past / Only what's done for Christ will last."
Today that phrase Marie loved and lived by is engraved on the
mantel above the fireplace in Hobby Lobby's conference center,
which we named the Legacy House. This is the place where our
family gathers one day each month to discuss business, another
day each month to celebrate birthdays, and once a year for a
celebration in which we revisit our family vision, mission, and
values. My (Jackie's) sister-in-law, Diana, and I were blessed to
be able to design the Legacy House, where multiple generations
of our family will meet and be reminded of this powerful quote
that is so important and is our family's legacy statement.

Let us share a full verse from that C. T. Studd poem Marie
was so fond of quoting.

Only one life, yes only one,
Soon will its fleeting hours be done;
Then, in "that day" my Lord to meet,
And stand before His Judgement seat;
Only one life, 'twill soon be past,
Only what's done for Christ will last.

Charles Thomas Studd was born in 1860 to a wealthy British businessman who had been saved at one of Dwight L. Moody's evangelistic crusade meetings. Charles himself became a believer while a boy, and he became a star cricket player at Britain's prestigious Eton College, then later at Trinity University in Cambridge. As a young man, Charles was one of the best-known athletes in all the British Empire. In the era before professional sports or the modern Olympic Games, the cricket teams of the British Empire were a public obsession and the centerpiece of national pride. C. T. Studd was a bona fide sports superstar in his day.

However, when one of his brothers became gravely ill and nearly died, the event had a tremendous, sobering impact on him. It forced Studd to consider the fragility and brevity of life. More important, it revealed how insignificant earthly wealth and prestige seem when one is faced with the prospect of entering eternity and giving an account of one's life. He realized that at the end of his life, money, popularity, or status would count for nothing. The only thing that would matter would be what he had done for Christ. This epiphany became the inspiration for his famous poem.

Out of his brother's health crisis came Charles's decision to become a missionary. Studd became one of the Cambridge Seven—a group of elite young men at Cambridge who volunteered themselves in the service of the famed missionary to China, Hudson Taylor. In 1885, at the age of twenty-four, Studd left England and joined Taylor's historic China Inland Mission.

There he met and married a British expat, and together

they brought four daughters into the world. After witnessing how unvalued and unwanted girls were in Chinese culture, Charles once wrote that he believed God gave him four consecutive daughters to demonstrate to the people there, through his delight, what a blessing baby girls are.[1]

While living in China, Charles inherited a trust fund fortune of twenty-nine thousand British pounds (roughly $25 million today). He kept none of the money, dividing it instead among a half dozen mission organizations and Christian charities for the poor, including the Moody Bible Institute in the US and George Müller's mission and orphanage in Bristol, England.

After ten years in China, health problems moved Charles and his family home to England for a season, and soon thereafter he sensed a missionary call to India. Four years of work there were followed by several decades in Africa, first in Sudan, then later in many parts of Africa. He died in 1931, in what was then called the Belgian Congo. He had served his Savior to the very end.

Studd famously wrote concerning his heart for missionary work in difficult places: "Some want to live within the sound of church or chapel bell; I want to run a rescue shop within a yard of hell."[2]

He had only one life to live, and he lived it well, and entered heaven, where a lifetime of spiritual treasure had been laid up for him. What is more, the rich tapestry of his legacy here on earth continues to be woven. It's astonishing to contemplate that, in a very real sense, we are one of the threads of that tapestry.

That thread ran through Studd's poem "Only One Life" and right through the heart of Marie Green, far away in the midwestern United States. The poem and Studd's example inspired her, and she used his words to help shape the character and values of her children, including David Green. Those values contributed to the extraordinary impact that he, Barbara, our family, and Hobby Lobby have had, and continue to have, for the cause of Christ around the world, including all that the Museum of the Bible will make possible for generations to come. Now it's our turn. And we feel the responsibility and opportunity resound through each day: How will we continue and broaden this legacy?

How will you build yours? What will you do that will "outlive your life"? The question isn't how many people notice or applaud today. As C. T. Studd, Marie Green, and all the extraordinary women of God we've spotlighted on these pages understood, there is a gracious God in heaven who notices and knows. The measure of influence and outcome is not up to us, but the everyday faithfulness is. Which is why, as we've illustrated through the lives of those we've highlighted here, legacy is not just for people who find themselves in the bright lights. It is not just for the elite few. Rather it is a calling for all of us. Legacy is for those of simple faith who show up every day and make their daily journey one of courage, witness, rescue, generosity, compassion, boldness, prayer, tenacity, teaching, loyalty, wisdom, and faith. The point is, we get to choose our legacy.

So often we believe the lie that what we do doesn't really make a difference. We would venture to say that the women whose lives we have examined and found to be inspiring and culture changing didn't feel that what they were doing every day would make a difference in society either. Their lives may have seemed mundane, but we all can name a woman or women in our lives who made a real impact on us. It is so easy to look at social media, at the entertainment world, or even at those around us and assume that living a meaningful and impactful life is for everyone else. It is time for each of us to figure out the things only *we* can do to be a legacy-leaving, intentional influencer with the people whom God places in our path.

These stories have inspired and challenged us. And as we've written this book, we realize that there are thousands and thousands more stories to be told. There are countless women reading these pages who are crafting their own stories of legacy, and there are still others who will be inspired to begin the next step of their legacy journey.

As you contemplate how to step into your legacy, we would suggest starting by thinking about the moments of your every day. Whatever you do, your every day matters! Whether it's changing diapers and cooking meals or preparing reports and sending emails, it matters. Our ordinary actions, after all, tell a story about our character, and our character shapes the world around us. As you weave kindness and faith into the mundane, every action becomes eternal.

Likewise, the big dreams God has placed in your heart matter too. When you say yes to what God is calling you to—no matter how daunting or scary it might seem—it matters.

You might feel like your legacy efforts are as tiny and insignificant as the two small coins the widow dropped into the offering that one day while Jesus was at the temple with His disciples. The gift may have been small, but Jesus saw it, and He praised her for it. The widow may have felt that those coins were not enough to give to God, but she gave them anyway. And as she dropped them in the offering, their little clinks echoed through eternity.

We have only this one life. We have only a few short years, yet as we take the next step of faith, and the next and the next, we believe that God will multiply our days and shape an eternal legacy. So, women of God, together let's be a generation of legacy-building leaders—of generosity and prayer, through loyalty and witness—wherever God calls us to go. A great adventure lies ahead! Let's each spend our one life using our gifts and strengths in His service. And the choice is yours: you can make this one life bold and beautiful, just as God created it to be. Because only what's done for Christ will last.

NOTES

INTRODUCTION

1. Brian Solomon, "Meet David Green: Hobby Lobby's Biblical Billionaire," *Forbes*, October 8, 2012, https://www.forbes.com/sites/briansolomon/2012/09/18/david-green-the-biblical-billionaire-backing-the-evangelical-movement/#3e49d4ea5807.
2. C. S. Lewis, *Mere Christianity* (Oxford: C. S. Lewis Pte. Ltd., 1952), 134.
3. Richard L. Dugdale, *The Jukes: A Study in Crime, Pauperism, Disease and Heredity: Also Further Studies of Criminals* (Boston: G. P. Putnam and Sons, 1877).
4. A. E. Winsnip, *Jukes-Edwards: A Study in Education and Heredity* (Harrisburg, PA: R. L. Myers and Co., 1900).
5. Max Lucado, *Outlive Your Life: You Were Made to Make a Difference* (Nashville: Nelson, 2010), title page.

CHAPTER 1: THE LEGACY OF COURAGE

1. Susan Jeffers, *Feel the Fear and Do It Anyway* (Boston, MA: Houghton Mifflin Harcourt, 1987), title page.
2. Holly Wagner, *Find Your Brave: Courage to Stand Strong When the Waves Crash In* (Colorado Springs, CO: WaterBrook, 2016), 8.
3. Keith Harper, ed., *Send the Light: Lottie Moon's Letters and Other Writings* (Macon, GA: Mercer Univ. Press, 2002), 89.
4. Ibid., 215.
5. Chuck Warnock, "Lottie Moon: The Facts and Myths about Her Life," EthicsDaily.com, August 16, 2011, *www.ethicsdaily.com/*

lottie-moon-the-facts-and-myths-about-her-life-cms-18369.
Accessed June 28, 2017.

6. Joni Eareckson Tada, "Breast Cancer #1: My Story,"
JoniandFriends.org, October 1, 2012, *www.joniandfriends.org/*
radio/4-minute/breast-cancer-1-my-story/. Accessed July 1, 2017.

7. "Joni Eareckson Tada: Breast Cancer Update," October 26, 2012,
PBS.org, *www.pbs.org/wnet/religionandethics/2013/06/07/october*
-26–2012-joni-eareckson-tada-breast-cancer-update/13587/.

8. Eareckson Tada, "Breast Cancer #1: My Story."

9. "Joni Eareckson Tada: Breast Cancer Update."

10. "Q&A with Joni Eareckson Tada," Preaching.com, *www*
.preaching.com/resources/articles/qa-with-joni-eareckson-tada/.
Accessed June 19, 2017.

11. Sir Edward Tyas Cook, *The Life of Florence Nightingale*, vol. 1
(London: Macmillan, 1914), 51.

12. Rick Warren, *The Purpose Driven Life: What on Earth Am I Here*
For? (Grand Rapids: Zondervan, 2002), 28.

CHAPTER 2: THE LEGACY OF GENEROSITY

1. *Words of Wisdom: 2700 Quotations for Writers, Speakers, and*
Leaders to Help Inspire, Encourage, and Guide (New York:
Gramercy, 1998), 58.

2. David Green and Bill High, *Giving It All Away . . . and Getting*
It All Back Again: The Way of Living Generously (Grand Rapids:
Zondervan, 2017), 77.

3. Mary Beth Chapman and Ellen Vaughn, *Choosing to SEE: A*
Journey of Struggle and Hope (Grand Rapids: Revell, 2010), 92.

4. Ibid., 93.

5. James R. Newby, *Elton Trueblood: Believer, Teacher, and Friend*
(New York: Harper and Row, 1990), 97.

CHAPTER 3: THE LEGACY OF WITNESS

1. Billy Graham, *The Secret of Happiness* (New York: Inspirational Press, 1995), 296.
2. David L. Larsen, ed., *The Company of the Preachers*, vol. 2 (Grand Rapids: Kregel, 1998), 728.
3. David W. Taylor, *Like a Mighty Army? The Salvation Army, the Church, and the Churches* (Cambridge, UK: James Clarke & Co., 2015), 59.
4. Catherine Bramwell-Booth, *Catherine Booth: The Story of Her Loves* (London: Hodder and Stoughton, 1970), 36.
5. Catherine Mumford Booth, *Papers on Aggressive Christianity* (London: S. W. Partridge, 1880), 8.
6. Marilyn Hickey, *Dinner with Muhammad: A Surprising Look at a Beautiful Friendship* (Lebanon, TN: Franklin Green, 2012), xiii.
7. Christopher Ash, *Marriage for God: Making Your Marriage the Best It Can Be* (Wheaton: Crossway, 2016), 180.

CHAPTER 4: THE LEGACY OF WISDOM

1. Lysa TerKeurst, *The Best Yes: Making Wise Decisions in the Midst of Endless Demands* (Nashville: Nelson, 2014), 45.
2. Catherine A. Brekus, *Sarah Osborn's World: The Rise of Evangelical Christianity in Early America* (New Haven: Yale Univ. Press, 2013), introduction.
3. Ibid., chapter 1.
4. Ibid., xv.
5. Sarah Young, *www.jesuscalling.com/author/*. Accessed September 1, 2017.
6. William Lyon Phelps, "Billy Phelps Speaking," *The Rotarian* 57, no. 4 (October 1940): 42.
7. Sue Donnelly, "The Gate of the Year—Minnie Louise Haskins," *LSE History*, London School of Economics, *http://blogs.lse.ac.uk/ lsehistory/2013/12/10/the-gate-of-the-year-minnie-louise-haskins -1875–1957/*. Accessed August 11, 2017.

8. Queen Elizabeth II, "A Speech by the Queen on the 40th Anniversary of Her Succession," November 24, 1992, *www.royal .uk/annus-horribilis-speech*. Accessed August 11, 2017.

9. Ibid.

10. Caroline Picard, "How the Queen Went to Extreme Lengths to Shield Her Grandsons after Diana's Death," *Good Housekeeping* (May 2017), *www.goodhousekeeping.com/life/news/a44424/queen -william-harry-diana-death/*. Accessed June 1, 2017.

11. *www.royal.uk/christmas-broadcast-2002*.

12. Queen Elizabeth II, "Christmas Broadcast 2000," December 25, 2000, *https://www.royal.uk/christmas-broadcast-2000*.

13. Ian Bradley, *God Save the Queen: The Spiritual Heart of the Monarchy* (New York: Bloomsbury, 2012), 179.

CHAPTER 5: THE LEGACY OF TEACHING

1. Dorothy Herrmann, *Helen Keller: A Life* (Chicago: Univ. of Chicago Press, 1999), 44.

2. Fidelia Fisk, *Recollections of Mary Lyon, with Selections from her Instructions to the Pupils in Mt. Holyoke Female Seminary* (Boston: American Tract Society, 1866), 20.

3. Ibid., 93.

4. Kay Arthur, *Our Covenant God: Living in the Security of His Unfailing Love* (Colorado Springs, CO: Waterbrook, 1999), 96.

CHAPTER 6: THE LEGACY OF RESCUE

1. Louis Giglio, foreword to Mary Francis Bowley, *The White Umbrella: Walking with Survivors of Sex Trafficking* (Chicago: Moody, 2012), xii–xiii.

2. Frances J. Crosby, "Rescue the Perishing" (1869), public domain.

3. Richard Durham, *Richard Durham's Destination Freedom: Scripts from Radio's Black Legacy, 1948–50* (Santa Barbara: Praeger, 1989), 70.

4. Rosemary Sadler, *Harriet Tubman: Freedom Seeker, Freedom Leader* (Toronto: Dundam, 2012), 147.

5. 1860 Census.

6. C. M. Joyner, "Modern-Day Slavery by the Numbers," *Relevant* (February 25, 2016), *https://relevantmagazine.com/reject-apathy/modern-day-slavery-by-numbers*.

7. Ibid.

8. "Restore at a Glance," *a21.org/content/reach-rescue-restore/gnjebd#restore*.

9. Max Lucado, foreword to Christine Cain, *Undaunted: Daring to Do What God Calls You to Do* (Grand Rapids: Zondervan, 2012), 11.

10. Christine Cain, *Undaunted: Daring to Do What God Calls You to Do* (Grand Rapids: Zondervan, 2012), 194.

CHAPTER 7: THE LEGACY OF COMPASSION

1. Francis Schaeffer, *Francis A. Schaeffer Trilogy* (Wheaton, IL: Crossway, 1990), 34.

2. Sir Edward Tyas Cook, *The Life of Florence Nightingale (Complete)*, Library of Alexandria, 1913.

3. Jacob Abbott, *The Corner-Stone: Or, A Familiar Illustration of the Principles of Christian Truth* (Boston: William Peirce, 1836), 86.

4. Mark Bostridge, *Florence Nightingale: The Making of an Icon* (New York: Macmillan, 2008), 54.

5. Sir Edward Tyas Cook, *The Life of Florence Nightingale*, vol. 1 (New York: Macmillan, 1914), 93.

6. Gillian Gill, *Nightingales: The Extraordinary Upbringing and Curious Life of Miss Florence Nightingale* (New York: Random House, 2007), 330.

7. Defend International, "UNICEF: More Than 26,000 Children under Five Die Every Day," January 23, 2008, *http://defendinternational.org/unicef-more-than-26000-children-under-5-die-every-day/*.

8. Saving Moses, "Full Annual Report: 2014," *savingmoses.org/ wp-content/uploads2015/05/SM_Annual_Rept_2014.pdf.*

CHAPTER 8: THE LEGACY OF BOLDNESS

1. Helen Keller, *The Open Door* (New York: Doubleday, 1957), 17.
2. Michael Anderson, "'No,'" *The New York Times Book Reviews 2000*, vol. 1 (New York: Taylor and Francis, 2001), 1334.
3. Ibid.
4. Ibid.
5. Ibid.
6. Joyce A. Hansen, *Rosa Parks: A Biography* (Santa Barbara: Greenwood, 2011), 41.
7. Katelyn Beaty, "Oxford's Unapologetic Female Apologist," *Christianity Today* (April 2015), http://www.christianitytoday .com/ct/2015/april/oxfords-unapologetic-female-apologist.html.
8. Ravi Zacharias, foreword to Amy Orr-Ewing, *Is the Bible Intolerant?* (Downers Grove, IL: InterVarsity Press, 2012).
9. Alister McGrath, endorsement in Amy Orr-Ewing, *Is the Bible Intolerant?* (Downers Grove, IL: InterVarsity Press, 2012).
10. Amy Orr-Ewing and Frog Orr-Ewing, *Millennials: Reaching and Releasing the Rising Generation* (Orton Southgate, Peterborough, UK: Upfront, 2010).
11. Beaty, "Oxford's Unapologetic Female Apologist."

CHAPTER 9: THE LEGACY OF TENACITY

1. Elisabeth Elliot, *Through Gates of Splendor: The Event That Shocked the World, Changed a People, and Inspired a Nation* (Peabody, MA: Hendrickson, 2010), 43.
2. Hank Moore, *Pop Icons and Business Legends: History of Commerce and Heritage of Culture* (New York: Morgan James, 2016), 246.
3. Angela Duckworth, *Grit: The Power of Passion and Perseverance* (New York: Simon and Schuster, 2016), 58.

4. "Fanny Crosby," Landmarks Preservation Society of Southeast (February 11, 2010), *http://landmarksse.org/fannycrosby.html*. Accessed September 21, 2017.

5. *The Hymn* (Hymn Society of America, 1984), version 35, p. 222.

6. Fanny Crosby, *Fanny Crosby's Life Story* (New York: Every Where, 1903), 27.

7. Ibid., 125.

8. Darlene Neptune, *Fanny Crosby Still Lives* (New Orleans: Pelican, 2001), 100.

9. Ibid., 94.

10. Fanny Crosby, "Blessed Assurance" (1873), public domain.

11. Catherine Grace O'Connell, "Lauren Scruggs Kennedy on Moving Past Loss and Finding Meaning in Life," ThriveGlobal.com, *https://journal.thriveglobal.com/an-interview-with-inspirational-influencer-lauren-scruggs-kennedy-d7ab8c200f9f*. Accessed August 8, 2017.

12. Jason Kennedy and Lauren Scruggs, *Your Beautiful Heart: 31 Reflections on Love, Faith, Friendship, and Becoming a Girl Who Shines* (Chicago: Tyndale Momentum, 2015), xi.

13. O'Connell, "Lauren Scruggs Kennedy on Moving Past Loss."

CHAPTER 10: THE LEGACY OF FAITH

1. Corrie ten Boom, *Jesus Is Victor* (Grand Rapids: Revell, 1985), 184.

2. Randolph S. Churchill, *Winston S. Churchill: Youth, 1874–1900* (Boston: Houghton Mifflin, 1966), 43.

3. Winston Churchill, *My Early Life: A Roving Commission* (London: Mandarin, 1930), 5.

4. Stephen Mansfield, *Never Give In: The Extraordinary Character of Winston Churchill* (Nashville: Cumberland House, 1996), 39.

5. Katherine T. Phan, "Hobby Lobby Founders Launch Bible Exhibit in Oklahoma," *Christian Post* (May 16, 2011), *www.christianpost.com/news/high-tech-robots-bring-bible-history-to-life-50259/*.

6. Peter Watson, "20 Rare Manuscripts in Astor Collection Going Up for Auction," *Chicago Tribune* (June 15, 1988), *http:// articles.chicagotribune.com/1988-06-15/entertainment/ 8801080419_1_psalter-manuscripts-british-library.*

CHAPTER 11: THE LEGACY OF PRAYER

1. Stormie Omartian, *Prayer Warrior: The Power of Praying Your Way to Victory* (Eugene, OR: Harvest House, 2013), 17.
2. "31 Prayer Quotes—Be Inspired and Encouraged!" Crosswalk .com, *www.crosswalk.com/faith/spiritual-life/inspiring-quotes/ 31-prayer-quotes-be-inspired-and-encouraged.html.* Accessed July 25, 2017.
3. John Wesley, *The Heart of Wesley's Journal*, ed. Ed Hughes and Hugh Price (Peabody, MA: Hendrickson, 2008), 127.
4. William Henry Fitchett, *Wesley and His Century: A Study in Spiritual Forces* (London: Smith, Elder & Co., 1906), 1.
5. Ibid.
6. Peter Matthews, *Who's Buried Where in London* (London: Bloomsbury, 2017), 37.
7. John Kirk, *The Mother of the Wesleys: A Biography* (Ambler, MA: Tresidder, 1864), vii.
8. M. P. Singh, *Quote Unquote (A Handbook of Quotations)* (New Delhi: Lotus Press, 2006), 229.
9. Adam Liptak, "Supreme Court Rejects Contraceptives Mandate for Some Corporations: Justices Rule in Favor of Hobby Lobby," *New York Times* (July 1, 2014), sec. US, 1.

CHAPTER 12: THE LEGACY OF LOYALTY

1. Caroline Fraser, *Prairie Fires: The American Dreams of Laura Ingalls Wilder* (New York: Henry Holt, 2017), 473.
2. Eric Felten, *Loyalty: The Vexing Virtue* (New York: Simon and Schuster, 2011), 2.
3. Steve Saint, *End of the Spear* (Chicago: Tyndale, 2010), 8–10.

4. Ruth Bell Graham, *Prodigals and Those Who Love Them* (Grand Rapids: Baker, 1991), 11.

5. Ruth Bell Graham, *Prodigals and Those Who Love Them: Words of Encouragement for Those Who Wait* (Grand Rapids, MI: Baker, 1999), 136.

6. Bill Bright and Vonette Bright, *The Greatest Lesson I've Ever Learned* (Orlando: New Life, 2005), 339.

CONCLUSION

1. Norman Grubb, *C. T. Studd: Cricketer and Pioneer* (Cambridge: Lutterworth Press, 1933), 122.

2. Tim Keesee, *Dispatches from the Front: Stories of Gospel Advance in the World's Difficult Places* (Wheaton: Crossway, 2014), 106.

FOREWORD BY RICK WARREN

HOW THE **BIBLE** HAS SHAPED OUR WORLD
AND WHY IT STILL MATTERS TODAY

THIS
DANGEROUS
BOOK

STEVE & JACKIE GREEN
FOUNDING FAMILY, MUSEUM OF THE BIBLE

WITH BILL HIGH

Available in stores and online!

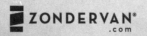

This Dangerous Book

How the Bible Has Shaped Our World and Why It Still Matters Today

Steve and Jackie Green with Bill High

THE BIBLE'S GREATEST DANGER LIES IN THE FACT THAT IT CHANGES LIVES

Avid collectors of biblical artifacts and the founders of the Museum of the Bible, Steve and Jackie Green explore the unique power of the Bible in this fascinating look at the world's most influential book.

In vivid detail, the Greens share the challenges they faced in acquiring biblical relics from around the world and why people—in every time and in every location—risked their lives to preserve this precious book.

The Greens explore ancient manuscripts, medieval commentaries, and modern biblical translations to give fascinating insights into the miracles and martyrdoms that led to the Scriptures we read today. The authors explain how cutting-edge technology gives new insight into the authenticity of the Bible, including the work of fifty scholars who uncovered hidden details about thirteen unpublished Dead Sea Scroll fragments. The Greens also look at the link between the Hebrew Bible and the New Testament, showing what we can learn from how the Bible was passed down to us, and why God's Word is foundational to America's past and crucial for its future.

The Bible is a world changer and a heart changer. Whether you have read the Bible for years or are simply curious about its influence, *This Dangerous Book* gives you a sense of wonder about the mystery, the power, and the legacy of God's Word.